ARCHAEOLOGIES OF
CONSCIOUSNESS

ARCHAEOLOGIES OF CONSCIOUSNESS

Essays in Experimental Prehistory

GYRUS

The fact that we find Lascaux beautiful means that Babylon has at last begun to fall.

Hakim Bey

DREAMFLESH PRESS

London

Published by Dreamflesh Press
BM 2374
London WC1N 3XX
England
http://dreamflesh.com

Dreamflesh Press is sort of an imprint of Strange Attractor ~ http://www.strangeattractor.co.uk

First print edition 2007

Dreamflesh Press serpent logo by Orryelle Defenestrate ~ http://www.crossroads.wild.net.au
Cover art: 'Ascension 2' by Andy Hemingway ~ http://www.ahgcreative.co.uk
Design and typography by Gyrus

Covers printed by Kennet Print on Forest Stewardship accredited card, using soya-based inks and Cellogreen compostable laminate. Unit 6, Hopton Industrial Estate, Devizes, Wiltshire SN10 2EU ~ 01380 720 049 ~ http://www.kennetprint.co.uk

Insides and binding by Antony Rowe. Bumper's Farm, Chippenham, Wiltshire SN14 6LH ~ 01249 659 705 ~ http://www.antonyrowe.co.uk

ISBN 0-9548054-7-X
ISBN-13 978-0-9548054-7-0

With grateful thanks to Paulus, Phil, Dave, Julian & Dorian, Holly, Debbie, Annexus, Iain, Orryelle, Donal, Paolo & Maura, Angelo, Mark, Andy and all contributors from themodernantiquarian.com. Special thanks to Albany for the doodle.

CONTENTS

Image credits

FOREWORD

OR THOSE MOST PERSISTENT and gifted independent truth seekers here in the secular West, only bodily death can bring to a conclusion the endless (and exhausting) tidal waves of startling insights and deep meaning that constantly bubble up and reveal themselves. Indeed, while the rest of the world sleeps on seemingly unperturbed, these Gnostic truth seekers almost grow used to being kept awake by their information overload; worse still for a select few the download of information persists even into their deepest dreams.

These Western truth seekers have no safety net of religion in which to seek solace, few sympathetic colleagues, and precious little respite do they get from their life's constant and sustained raw interface with the unknown. Unlike their equivalent mystical neighbours in the Middle- and Far East, whose cultures have retained most of their epic oral traditions and colossal libraries of arcane ideas, these Western researchers are out on their own, as successive generations of Christian priests took it upon themselves to destroy our local ancestral wisdom in preference for the Monotheistic Judeo-Christian thoughts emanating from the so-called Holy Land.

Gyrus is just one of these gifted and highly independent Western truth seekers, but I believe him to be one of the very best. In the twelve years that we've been close friends, his research, his writing and his publication schedules have been nothing short of heroic. During that time, he's lived in Leeds, Bristol and London, and spent long periods of time studying first-hand prehistoric monuments and rock art, as well as marshalling enormous amounts of raw material for umpteen articles, and editing together other adepts' insights for his four-part project *Towards 2012*.

Like all my favourite researchers, however, there are no limits to where Gyrus finds the truth, and even "dreams, drugs [and] conversations with truckers who give me lifts" can act as a springboard to new research for this most open-minded of thinkers. But sustaining any successful artistic life that requires achieving regular heightened states is always problematic, and most who try eventually fall from such a programme. Not so with Gyrus, I believe. He's unearthed (and is still unearthing) far too much essential stuff to stop now. Indeed, were the world to come to an end tomorrow and with no one left to confide in, Gyrus would most likely still bring forth his fascinating… nay, essential opinions—if only for the sake of his own personal mental health.

For his writing alone, Gyrus is worthy of our trust. But for his superb and enduring research, he is worthy of our deep gratitude.

JULIAN COPE
THE MARLBOROUGH DOWNS

INTRODUCTION

I HAD MY KNIFE. My intent was clear, and the stone with its ancient glyphs lurked in the distance across the grassy, rugged moor.

The Badger Stone on Rombald's Moor, near Ilkley in West Yorkshire, had been the site of my misty initiation into this lore-riddled landscape[1], so it seemed like an appropriate focus for initiating the next wave of my investigations. I wanted to ask the goddess of the River Wharfe, into which the north side of this moor pours its babbling waters, for inspiration in researching her history. Verbeia, a Romano-Celtic deity intimately associated with Ilkley, the Wharfe and—I intuited playfully—the moor's odd rock carvings, was quite opaque to me at the time. I knew her basics from Anne Ross's *Pagan Celtic Britain*, but I wasn't aware at the time that Verbeia's association with the very similar goddess Brighid made it probable that she presided over (among other things) poetry and writing.

I started to feel the familiar excitement and slight nervousness that builds as you approach a solo working in an uninhabited landscape. The grey sky was gathering itself, and I felt spots of rain on my face. By the time I reached the stone, its pale grey millstone grit, smothered in meandering archaic carvings, was turning dark from the increasingly heavy downpour. The harsh southerly wind was pelting the shower at an ever-shallower angle, and the heavy drops of rain were steadily becoming lashes of bitter hail. The little specks of ice danced skittishly as they hit the rock surface.

Gathering my focus, I got my knife out of my bag, readied my plasters, and positioned myself before one of the large basins at the top of this rough, belly-high boulder. This basin seems to have been worn into the stone naturally, but it has a clearly artificial channel carved down from its lower lip, alongside the other lines and glyphs, suggest-

1. See p. 70.

ing liquid flows. I chanted and spoke my requests to Verbeia with the hail coursing past me from behind, its near-horizontal angle creating a strange tunnel-like vortex effect. I slit my finger open and dripped my blood offering into the stone receptacle.

Applying my plaster, the hail ebbed back to heavy rain; closing the ritual and walking away, the rain slowed, lightened, then stopped... and the wind returned to a light breeze.

THE NEXT FEW MONTHS were a vertiginous flurry of books, insights and synchronicity. Here isn't the place for a searching wrangle with you, dear reader, over whether magic is "real" or not (it's debatable whether anywhere is such a place). Suffice it to say, experiments with ritual, altered states, dreamwork and general larking about with consciousness have formed an integral part of my study of prehistory.

The first thing to be said about this approach is that it's a large net, trawling through deep waters. It can bring a bewildering array of ideas and connections to the surface. They can flap around gasping in a disconcerting way while you decide what to do with them, and some of them bite.

A kind of wallowing, scattershot approach to sorting through them is often initially necessary (and fun!), just to crack that bewildered standoffishness that such bounties can induce. But it's been of great interest to me that once this slippery ecstasy subsides, you often discover some truly significant specimens among your catch. Odd, captivating things that rarely see the light, but which somehow fail to wholly slip back into the darkness once beheld. The immediate result of the ritual described above—the essay 'The Goddess in Wharfedale', presented here—was an outpouring of rich, bewitching perceptions. But after some cooking, stewing, and refining, I found that I ended up with some solid contributions to the local history of the region. Published as *Verbeia: Goddess of Wharfedale* under the name G.T. Oakley, this distillation seemed to act as a vaguely respectable validation of my earlier, more personal and "gnostic"[2] approach.

This apparently neat trajectory, from a wild storming of the brain to sober publication, belies a tension running through these writings, between the freewheeling excitement of gnostic research, and the lesser, but nevertheless present urge to have my ideas accepted more by our arbiters of knowledge. Much of my antipathy to academia has softened over the years, as I've met open-minded academics and grown to respect their often impressive accomplishments and dedication. Yet my passion for more wayward paths to knowledge has remained; even as I gain respect for many academic scholars, I

---

2. I use a small 'g' here to imply a general emphasis on personal, inner apprehension; no direct reference to Gnosticism, the early Christian heresy, is implied.

realize that I am probably bound—in these writings, at least—to an even more obscure niche than theirs. This kind of esoteric exploration is open to all, but not for everyone.

This collection is presented in the knowledge that its appeal may be limited, but in the firm belief that there is a vital place for the ideas and approaches it represents in our cultural ecology. Occult philosopher Ramsey Dukes has suggested the formation of a "Crank's Union",

> *to improve self image by dwelling on the positive benefits of crankdom. To admit that it is exciting to be a crank; to recognise the thrill of seeing sudden connections of meaning between unrelated phenomena; to pit oneself against vertigo on the brink of the unknown, and then to jump.*[3]

In the same way that the chaotic, inexorable processes of natural evolution will never be wholly subsumed under some controlled project of genetic engineering concocted by the human ego, this kind of crazy, indulgent exploration, allowing contradiction and worshipping glitches, will always find a space for itself. It may be of some use to more rational, positivist quests for knowledge, but it will never be their slave.

ANIMIST "MAGIC" DOES HAVE its rational justifications. The practice, habit or tradition of relating to some other-than-human entities in the world—animals, plants, rocks, weather—as *persons* was of course initially taken by modern learning as "primitive superstition". Early anthropologists, studying indigenous cultures after their own had purged their animist tendencies through the brutalizations of monotheism and science, adopted a patronizing tone at best.

However, in *The Prehistory of the Mind*, Steven Mithen makes an excellent case for the idea that this sort of tendency actually forms the *basis* of human consciousness. He draws on the "modular" theory of the mind, which sees cognitive processes divided into several key modules or domains, i.e. Social Intelligence, Technical Intelligence, Natural History Intelligence, etc. He sees some evidence for each in the meagre remains left by early hominids, but contests that the crucial leap made by *Homo sapiens* was to allow multi-directional flows of knowledge and perception *between* these domains. Thus, the Technical Intelligence used to make tools is co-opted by Social Intelligence, and the ever-complexifying stream of socially significant artifacts (e.g. jewellery) bursts forth. Likewise, the apprehension of the environment that Natural History Intelligence rep-

3. From 'On Writing and Publishing: A Crank's Progress', in *What I Did In My Holidays* (TMTS and Mandrake of Oxford, 1998).

resents became thoroughly imbued with Social Intelligence; the ecology in which we are embedded is not seen as a simple realm of 'otherness', but is sentient, populated with persons. Our relations to the world are conditioned by our ways of relating to other humans, and our human relations are laden with patterns and images from nature.

Social Intelligence is crucial. A common, and good, idea brought to bear on the origins of human consciousness points to the large size of the human social group in comparison to its hominid forebears. More people in the group means exponentially rising levels of complexity in social interactions, and hence greater demands on your poor grey matter. Brain size can generally be correlated to social group size. And much of this extra hardware is used for increasingly complex "theory of mind" software. That is, the part of your mind that manages to model the minds around it. Deft social interactions depend on how well you can second-guess other people—whether you're needing to love them or deceive them. In relating to people, it's very useful to have as clear a representation as possible of their head-state. It's even more useful to have a clue about *their* representation of *your* head-state.

It seems to me that Social Intelligence (if we take this simplistic but useful "modular" approach) often informs other domains of knowledge more than *vice versa*. So much evolutionary effort has been expended on developing our Social Intelligence (though you wouldn't know it sometimes), it's simply efficient to apply those skills in attention, perception, and reaction to other arenas—like the environment.

Darwinian theory tells us that this application of "people skills" to "other-than-human people" must have evolved as an adaptive advantage in the frequently harsh environments our forebears thrived in. Its manifestation in mature adult populations shouldn't be misconstrued, with that patronizing Victorian tone, as some unfortunate fallacy that persists a child's natural, playful anthropomorphisms. There would have been little room for childish wrong-headedness during ice ages. In fact, when you stop to think about it, it seems more likely that the cushy conditions of our present Holocene interglacial have fostered ultimately maladaptive luxuries of the mind.

Ethnographic evidence about the beliefs of the dwindling remnants of modern-day foraging cultures are often brought to bear on models of the prehistoric mind, alongside the scraps of archaeological data we have. Some argue that it's a false leap of induction to assume that early humans related to the environment in the same way as present-day indigenous cultures. Indeed, we need to respect the important distinctions between them. However, all the evidence—and most scholars—point to some variation of animism as the dominant *modus operandi* of humans up until a few thousand years ago. It's an effective survival tool, evolved over hundreds of thousands of years. Such deep stretches of time are the only real yardstick for scoring evolutionary points; the idea that our recent few millennia of toying with abstract faith and rational logic have somehow utterly trumped this profound evolutionary heritage is—despite modern technology's quantitative achievements thus far—a little premature, to say the least.

The stream of history that gushed out from the birth of agriculture and civilization wasn't a cascade of inevitable superiority. These essays are often concerned with the metal ages and the Neolithic—my gateways back to the pre-monotheist past. But it should be recognized that the shift from Palaeolithic foraging to Neolithic farming entailed as tremendous and violent a rewiring of the psyche as that later tumultuous shift from paganism to the religions of the Book. After farming came into being through a particular confluence of post-glacial environmental factors,

> *Farmers needed to expand into new territories, before their old lands gave out and died. We have no reason to believe that this expansion happened peacefully. The idea that agriculture spread peacefully, as hunter-gatherers recognized the ease it brought, seems preposterous given what we know now from the archaeological record. Finds … show that agriculture led to severe and sudden malnutrition, disease, and a much abbreviated lifespan. It involved a great deal more labor, far less leisure time, and significant compromises of health.*[4]

It also created surplus, severe social divisions, and greater military might. Rather than being adopted due to its obvious benefits for its members, civilization spread largely through the self-perpetuating force of its own large-scale powers. As we come to terms with its ecological short-sightedness, we will be forced to reconsider—or spontaneously rediscover—the subtle powers of the traditions we've tried to wipe off face of the Earth. Animism's not dead.

Uncle Ramsey is once more to hand with shrewd observations, in his *Little Book of Demons*,[5] in which he uses the example of attending to a broken photocopier:

> *… [P]eople confuse two different things: sense and logic. It is certainly not logical to assume the copier has a mind, when there is no evidence of neural activity, of communication, or of the level of complexity associated with mental processes. Logic does have some place in magical thinking, but its role is subservient and it is certainly true that science is far more logical than magic.*
>
> *On the other hand, magic is far more sensible than science because it is an ap-*

4. http://anthropik.com/2007/09/a-short-history-of-western-civilization/ (by Jason Godesky)
5. *Little Book of Demons* by Ramsey Dukes (Aeon, 2005).

plication of all the senses. When we think of a copier as a conscious being, instead of a mechanical object, we are vastly expanding our sensibilities to embrace mood, purpose, affection, commitment and a multidimensional infinitude of additional factors. The copier could be malfunctioning because it is an undercover agent for a rival organisation, it might be a revolutionary fanatic wishing to sabotage the business, it might simply hate me, or it might equally have fallen in love with me and be trying to attract my attention…

The possibilities are endless, they are highly illogical, but they are all simultaneously embraced by that single process of personification.

The tiny trickle of mental activity represented by logical thought has expanded into a torrent of parallel processes as the brain gears up to tackle the most challenging object in the universe—a fellow conscious being.

The logical mindset has such a rigid dominance over many of us that carefully crafted reframings such as this are useful and often necessary to tease us back to our animist inheritance. And the initial steps of this renaissance, for the individual and the collective, are often clumsy; our cultural assumption that animism is childish forgets that, in its mature form, it is a fantastically sophisticated way of being, requiring as much (if not more) sustained persistence to properly rekindle as science does to be learned. It is easy to dive into, but usually very difficult to attain any measure of graceful competence. As Jim Morrison said of the move away from voyeuristic consciousness, "Whenever we seek to break this spell of passivity, our actions are cruel and awkward and generally obscene, like an invalid who has forgotten how to walk."[6]

All this notwithstanding, its re-emergence seems both fruitful and inevitable to me. As our lack of attentiveness to and respect for the environment rebounds catastrophically in the form of the Sixth Great Extinction, climate chaos, and the collapse of the ecological basis for our civilization in fossil fuels, fertile soil and drinkable water… Well, either we rebuild this relationship consciously or we'll be forced into a brutal, pared-back relationship of fumbling necessity.

And right at the heart of this revival, however much we need to justify it rationally, is the experiential leap—the moment of actually *doing* it. Whether or not rocks, animals, plants, ancient monuments or patterns of weather are "actually" conscious, the triggering of this living relationship only really kicks in when you act *as if* they are. Pushing past feelings of foolishness, fear and awkwardness, you get glimpses of life and significance permeating the world. And pushing past derision and paranoia, you start

6. From his poem 'The Lords'.

to grow sustained, nourishing relationships.

THE STUDY OF PREHISTORY seems a little trivial next to the collapse of civilization. But then again, don't many things? At least studying prehistory—unlike most trivia that our lives revolve around—only *seems* insignificant in this context. Actually, it provides exactly the kind of grounds for sharper self-knowledge and awareness of our place in the broad sweep of time that is now demanded.

Steven Mithen reflects in *After the Ice* on Paul Theroux's "desire to experience 'otherness to its limit'" through travel, and "how becoming a stranger allowed him to discover who he was and what he stood for." Mithen goes on to note:

As globalisation leads to a bland cultural homogeneity throughout the world, imaginative travel to prehistoric times is perhaps the only way we can now acquire that extreme sense of otherness by which we recognise ourselves.

I would add that although reflective reading is a wonderful form of travel, this imaginative journeying can also be *enacted* through engaged, experimental activity in the world, inspired by the very cultures under study. Although there is no question of "going back", this participative approach can expand on Theroux's self-definition through "otherness" with the perception of the *commonalities* that still weave through time and space to form our shared human identity.

Thanks to its largely cumulative nature and our eagerness for more and more shiny gadgets, science is reflexively associated with the future; but one of its greatest achievements has been the demolition of our extensive monotheism-induced *amnesia*. Geology and natural history smashed the Church's insistence on a relatively short, relatively static lifetime for creation. In a reversal of the existential shock experienced by the replicants in *Blade Runner*, when they discover their childhood has been implanted, we still reel from the revelation that our species and the world has a *much* deeper past than we even suspected.

Eviatar Zerubavel, in his useful book *Time Maps: Collective Memory and the Social Shape of the Past*, notes that "as exemplified by the traditional image of the creation of the world *ex nihilo*, we tend to envision beginnings as preceded by actual void." Science uncovers ever more information on the deep past, like psychoanalysis unravelling occluded episodes and feelings from childhood; yet the desire to forget or to wipe clean the past remains strong. Zerubavel quotes leading Zionist Bert Katznelson as saying:

We cultivate oblivion and are proud of our short memory. ... And the depth of our insurrection we measure by our talent to forget. ... The more rootless we see ourselves, the more we believe that we are more free, more sublime. ... It is roots that delay our upward growth.

This kind of utopian flight from the past is, I believe, precisely what has led us to our present ecological and social impasse. Just as we have ravaged and destabilized the ecologies of living forms that interpenetrate across spatial bioregions, our culture's anxious longing for a clean slate has devastated our temporal roots. There is no greater world-historical irony to illustrate this than the current havoc being wreaked upon the remains of Sumerian civilization in Iraq.[7] Industrial civilization's rabid energy needs are leading to the large-scale sacking of the remnants of one of its most important historical milestones.

PSYCHOLOGIST JAMES HILLMAN has said that Classical history "gave the Renaissance imagination a place to put archetypal structures—gave it a structure within which to fantasize."[8] Likewise, prehistoric monuments and art, and their relations to modern hunter-gatherer cultures, give the 'Archaic Revival'[9] "a structure within which to fantasize". Our few archaeological facts provide a skeletal basis for our vision of the past, but imagination must flesh things out. This "bounded speculation", as I've come call it, is ever-shifting, as the borderlands of "fact" and "imagination" are constantly being negotiated, personally and socially.

But what if we are deluded? What if, like hopelessly amateur palaeontologists, we reconstruct absurd, unreal creatures from incomplete skeletons, creatures which bear little resemblance to the skeleton's actual owner? My response is, let's embrace all possibilities. There is no need to dispense with our critical faculties; indeed, in these uncertain realms we need them more than ever. But our criticism should also be turned on itself from time to time. Perpetual caution may be "safer"; but fun, inspiration, and the more bizarre tastes of the soul also deserve space. The underpinning structures of the past that archaeology can substantiate should be respected; but to just leave them be, guarded by a cold, "This is all we can know", both disrespects imagination and leaves us prey to the potential for seeing the past as a mere skeleton—truly dead and desiccated. Spartan, inanimate memories are surely little better than amnesia.

7. See http://news.independent.co.uk/fisk/article2970762.ece
8. *Re-Visioning Psychology.*
9. A term coined by the late Terence McKenna.

GIVEN THE PREMISES of this book, as I approached the writing of this introduction I realized some act of remembrance was necessary. I returned to Avebury in Wiltshire, a place which has inspired me immensely, and slept in the Neolithic tomb at West Kennet to ask for dreams.

I placed my offerings of a bread roll and an apple in the main chamber at the rear,[10] and, having requested a dream to guide this writing, settled down to sleep in one of the smaller chambers. The unfeasible silence and darkness kept me awake for a while, along with the occasional shower outside, a mouse scampering across my head, and odd noises near the front that always sounded like people…

In my dream, I entered a comic shop in a basement. While looking for graphic novels about magical theory, I happened across a curious hand-crafted A6 grimoire about a Great Old One.[11] All its text was formed by the characters being cut out of sheets of gold leaf stuck to mauve or black card. "This must have been expensive to put together," I thought; then I noticed the £37 price tag on the back.

This dream seemed to present some practical advice about not sparing expenses in the production of this book (though I'm sure you're glad I didn't take the pricing literally). But further levels of meaning were suggested by my coincidental discovery, immediately after returning home from Avebury, of a new blog called *The Fabulous Forager*.[12] A playful attempt to counter the Hobbesian "nasty, brutish, and short" vision of "primitive" life with anthropological and primitivist perspectives on fashion and beauty, the concept of the blog resonated deeply for me after my dream. Was the barrow not urging me to pay attention to the *aesthetic* aspect of prehistory?

Prehistoric art is indeed a core theme here. Perhaps, in imaginatively investigating the origins and purposes of archaic art, we can discover something about our own artistic traditions, our own sense of beauty. Art in tribal cultures lacks the segregated, framed context that we're so used to when confronting aesthetic creativity; it acts as a vital manifest hub for the invisible forces of feeling, thought and memory that bind a culture together, and it permeates lived life. And more than fostering cultural coherence, it binds culture to nature. Culture is seen to grow out of nature as plants grow from the soil.

Beyond the social function of art, though, we might also pay attention to the real

10. I cleared them away in the morning and disposed of them. I find the belief that spirits eat the "essence" of food offerings, which can be thrown away elsewhere post-ceremony, useful in avoiding the unsightly littering of ancient monuments.
11. A being from H.P. Lovecraft's Cthulhu Mythos stories.
12. http://anthropik.com/fabulousforager/ (by Giulianna Maria Lamanna)

meaning of "aesthetics". Sidelined by our religious puritanism and our functional scientism, aesthetic appreciation often becomes an indulgence, an airy distraction. The original Greek, *aisthesis*, though, refers to "sensual perception". Here we may find an earthy discrimination, a careful attention to texture and detail that has as much to do with science as art and magic. It suggests concreteness rather than abstraction.

Abstraction has its place, of course, and here I give it plenty of room to play in. But I've also endeavoured to give more space than is usual to my concrete experiences, my sensual, unpredictable interactions with the living world (including the inner worlds of autonomous form in dreams and visions). For many of us, as much as "aesthetics" have floated off into nebulous irrelevance, "concreteness" has hardened into grey rigidity. Our lumpen modern architectural concrete stands as an emblem of the calcification of our sensual engagement with the world. From the Latin for "grow together", *concrete* implies tangible manifestation; but the word has lost its original suggestion of merging ecological complexity.

The concrete world and the aesthetic sense need to be rejoined, and the common thread is beauty—a felt awe wherein perception seizes the heart and expands our apprehension. In cultures with strong currents of puritanism in their recent past, the current waves of glossy, mass-mediated aestheticism are just cruel, awkward and obscene steps towards beauty; still a far cry from genuinely bringing beauty back into everyday life. This surface sheen of conventionalized glamour needs to be shattered by opening up to what Terence McKenna always called "the felt presence of immediate experience"—a domain of shifting surprises that, if enough attention is paid to it, perpetually confounds the scientific and commercial desire for *repeatability*.

The pre-monotheist realm of embodied spirituality, magical art and living visions is a crucial source of inspiration for this reawakening. We need to discover that precious, hand-crafted grimoire in the basement.

GYRUS

STROUD GREEN, LONDON, AUTUMN 2007

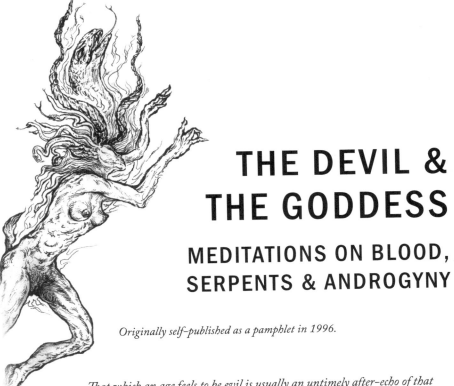

THE DEVIL & THE GODDESS

MEDITATIONS ON BLOOD, SERPENTS & ANDROGYNY

Originally self-published as a pamphlet in 1996.

That which an age feels to be evil is usually an untimely after-echo of that which was formerly felt to be good—the atavism of an older ideal.

Friedrich Nietzsche

THE FOLLOWING WRITINGS began as a short article written in reaction to numerous interviews I had read with 'Satanic' or 'black metal' bands (in *Esoterra* magazine). I got very tired of their knee-jerk social Darwinism, their philosophy of "the strong over the weak". Metal bands will never be the best exponents of any philosophy, and Satanism shouldn't be judged according to their interviews. Nevertheless, their simplistic view of nature's laws (which in any case should be seen as nature's *habits*) encapsulate many quibbles I have with the social Darwinist shades of Satanism, and occultism in general. There are a lot of much more enlightened strains of the 'left-hand path', as these writings will hint at. These strains usually attempt to transcend the left/right dualism of occult morality, a false dichotomy where self-interest and concern for others are seen to be mutually exclusive.

While I'm not a Satanist, occult philosophies have a deep influence on my world-view and life. I read widely on these subjects, and though I love toying with ideas, maps and models for intellectual amusement, I find that I'm with Nietzsche when he says, "I do not know what purely intellectual problems are." So what began as a somewhat playful little jab at the shaky foundations of social Darwinism gradually evolved into an outpouring of the visions and intuitions that my recent experiences, research and reflection have led me to. It's an exorcism of sorts, an attempt to externalize the insights, feelings and perceptions that I often find flooding into me, seemingly unbidden, but later seen to be exactly what I needed to shift my world-view out of a stale or narrow perspective. I find it's only through externalizing these cascades of insight that I can make room for more to arrive.

My research is not strictly 'scholarly'. Dreams, drugs, sex, conversations with truckers who give me lifts, synchronicity-laden trails that lead me to books I wouldn't usually notice, trashy movies, walks in the countryside, emotional breakdowns, lazy days, playing with kids... all these play a more significant role in the evolution of my ideas than the traditional academic activities of 'thinking' and 'reading'. And, when I really look at it, I can't imagine that this is anything new. Life isn't cut into categories in the way that the division of academia into different disciplines pretends it is. Everything influences everything else, and I think what I'm doing is just consciously recognizing this... and then writing.

That said, some of the material here is quite 'dense', laden with associations which might come to me, immersed as I am in it all, without much effort, but which may ask a lot more of the reader than passive word-by-word consumption. As far as this sort of writing goes, I try to tread a precarious path between making myself clear and passionately wanting to be a 'sounding board'. I want to leave gaps, be oblique, allow space for the reader to enter into my thoughts, fuse with them to an extent, and come away with more than 'information'. I'm not in the business of handing people complete, air-tight systems of ideas on a plate. I don't think you can show something to someone that they haven't already seen; but I know from my own experience that we've all seen a lot more than we often pretend. I want to try to help people remember this. Also, the nature of the areas dealt with here means that words can never present a view of them that is even close to being 'complete'. All they can do is suggest, trigger, and point. Exactly what they will suggest, trigger off or point to will depend on who you are and where you are. Ideally, you'll take more of yourself away from this than you will of me.

Many of the ideas here utterly contradict beliefs I held two years ago. I don't doubt that two years from now I'll be off somewhere else. As Alan Watts said, "I am not one who believes that it is any necessary virtue in the philosopher to spend his life defending a consistent position. It is surely a kind of spiritual pride to refrain from 'thinking out loud', and to be unwilling to let a thesis appear in print until you are prepared to champion it to the death." This doesn't mean I don't want people to criticize this writing. Yes, these are my present opinions, but they will change—and I only got *here* by having my opinions challenged, as well as 'confirmed' by experiences and other people. I never want this process to stop.

There are several different, but subtly related parts to these writings. I call them "meditations" because although there are clear conceptual threads weaving throughout the different sections, there is no attempt at a coherent 'argument'. Parts of it relate to and reflect off others parts in ways I never anticipated; no doubt many of the intended resonances will fall flat. As I said before, language, being linear, just can't accurately describe the ideas and modes of experience I'm dealing with. All I can do is spin words, my own and the sampled words of others, around these things, revealing a fragment here, a fragment there, but still leaving mere fragments. Each trying to describe the same underlying thing, each reflecting a different part of it, in the hope that a multitude of linear perspectives can come closer to representing this non-linear vision.

Firstly, there are some arguments about the philosophical underpinnings of what has come to be known as Satanism in modern occulture. This section, being the original seed-article, could stand on its own, but hopefully the reader will soon see its intimate relevance to the other meditations as they're unravelled. Then, taking its cue from the ubiquitous urge to uncover spiritual fertility buried beneath centuries of Christian domination, there is a speculative look at the genesis of the Devil—and what lies beyond.

The Devil & The Tao

As far as the philosophical underpinnings of Satanism go, one of the best places to start is with Friedrich Nietzsche. While he had nothing (consciously) to do with Satanism, his work is frequently cited by Satanists and modern occultists, and I think more than a few Satanists see themselves as 'Nietzschean'.

It has to be said before setting off that Nietzsche was acutely, probably painfully aware of how his ideas may be misinterpreted. He loathed the idea that people, "like plundering troops", may pick and choose titbits from his books to use for their own purposes, disregarding material contrary to their own agendas. The racist misinterpretations (far too weak a word!) of the German Nazi party are the most blatant case in point. That said, I disagree with some of his work. In the end Nietzsche was no 'system-builder'—he erected no edifice that must be accepted entirely or fall to the ground. He was an *experimentalist*, and perpetually played with and revised ideas. It is in this spirit that I read Nietzsche; and here I'm looking at him with an eye to reveal a few misinterpretations less obvious than those of the half-witted anti-Semites. No doubt I'll end up guilty of a bit of plundering myself, but I prefer judicious plunder to wilful misunderstanding.

Darwinism is the central concept to deal with. It amuses me to see 'black metal' bands asked in interviews if they believe in the (supposedly 'Nietzschean') philosophy of "the strong over the weak", "survival of the fittest"—as if this would provoke some new and interesting response! We're talking *social* Darwinism here of course, but let's look first at the biological argument.

Darwinian evolutionary theory often seems too obvious to bother arguing with, but this is precisely my problem with it. It's too bloody obvious. The nail was whacked on the head for me when I read Arthur Koestler's *Janus: A Summing Up*. Here he quotes C.H. Waddington, a critical neo-Darwinian:

> *Survival does not, of course, mean the bodily endurance of a single individual, outliv-ing Methuselah. It implies, in its present-day interpretation [1957], perpetuation as a source for future generations. That individual 'survives' best which leaves most offspring. Again, to speak of an animal as 'fittest' does not necessarily imply that it is strongest or most healthy or would win a beauty competition. Essentially it denotes nothing more than leaving most offspring. The general principle of natural selec-tion, in fact, merely amounts to the statement that the individuals which leave most offspring are those which leave most offspring. It is a tautology.*

Further, Ludwig von Bertalanffy acutely observes that "It is hard to see why evolu-tion has ever progressed beyond the rabbit, the herring, or even the bacterium which are unsurpassed in their reproductive capacities."[1]

The so-called rationalism of modern—usually 'socially Darwinian'—Satanism rests on very dodgy philosophical ground, simply because when you bother to try and define the terms used in the idea of "the strong over the weak", you're invariably left with a sense of, "Yeah, and…?" It's like saying you believe in the philosophy of "winners beating the losers". Jello Biafra nicely undermined knee-jerk social Darwinism with

---

1. Is this the right question? Maybe instead of asking why nature evolved past the bacterium, we should ask, "Why not?" [2007]

his quip that "the strong prey on the weak, and the clever prey on the strong"; but in the end this just begs the question. Also, orthodox Darwinism inevitably holds that humanity is the latest in life's progressively 'better' attempts at creating organisms.[2] Surely social Darwinism would hold a similar view about contemporary culture? This doesn't sit too well with the misanthropy, and contempt for the 'lowering of standards' in modern society, that is prevalent among many supposed social Darwinists. If the strong really do overpower the weak, why have we been dominated for so long by such a half-assed religion as Christianity? I think many Satanists, in claiming "strong over the weak" to be a universal principle of nature, are actually trying to say, "I'm harder than you and I could have you easily." Or at least, "I could out-stare you, mate." That's another argument. But as for universal principles—forget it. Evolution and history are far too complex and multi-dimensional to limit themselves to the strategies of a fight in a pub.

Nietzsche was definitely not a Darwinist, and had no faith in "survival of the fittest" as an 'explanation'. For him, his conception of the "will to power" was the driving force behind all life. It is essentially a conception of creativity, and has far more to do with creative self-mastery than power over others. Nietzsche's notion that creation must be destructive ("Who wishes to be creative, must first destroy and smash accepted values.") is often seen in limited terms. This is only the first step. The second step, often left out, is that the new creation itself must again be destroyed. And the steps go on... Zarathustra is quite explicit on this: "And life itself told me this secret: 'Behold,' it said, 'I am that *which must overcome itself again and again...*'" The famous 'Superman' isn't a concept of some inevitable evolutionary goal toward which humanity is inexorably moving (i.e. it's not Darwinian). It's a vision of an ideal *state of being*, of perfect self-mastery and perpetual re-creation, which Nietzsche believed some humans—Socrates and Goethe for example—had already, to an extent, achieved. Together with his doctrine of eternal recurrence, it's a glorification of the moment, of total involvement in the turbulent flow of immediate experience. "*Not to wish to see too soon.*— As long as one lives through an experience, one must surrender to the experience and shut one's eyes instead of becoming an observer immediately. For that would disturb the good digestion of the experience: instead of wisdom one would acquire indigestion." (*The Wanderer and His Shadow*)

Comparison with Taoism is illuminating. While our cultural filters place Taoism in some 'soft' category, and see Nietzschean values as being essentially 'hard', the distinc-

---

2. This is popular, not orthodox Darwinism. See Mary Midgley's *Evolution as a Religion*. [2007]

tion blurs when you consider the supra-cultural state to which both aspire. Nietzsche used the word 'hard' many times in describing ideals, as in "all creators are hard." (*Twilight of the Idols*) But I don't think we can just accept this word unquestioningly. Its modern connotations evoke more of a mindless thug than a vibrant Superman. Words are subject to mutation; but even if the words themselves remain the same, their meaning is always mutating, for words are "pockets into which now this and now that has been put, and now many things at once." (*The Wanderer and His Shadow*)

Before considering Taoism, I'd like to follow a little tangent about Nietzsche's 'hardness'. I always thought of Nietzsche (before actually reading him) as some grim Teutonic beast. He was actually vehemently opposed to the Germanic temperament, which he considered mediocre (when in a good mood). He repeatedly praised the southern European disposition, that of light-heartedness, exuberance and cheerfulness. A far cry from the fashionably serious and dreary poses of many modern 'Nietzscheans'. A key influence on this popular misconception of Nietzsche is probably that famous portrait—the furrowed brow, the dark gaze, the amazingly bushy moustache. It doesn't do much for his philosophy of light-heartedness. I was tempted to just put this image, of a very stern and worried-looking guy, down to his frequent bouts of illness. I recently found out that I was more justified in this temptation than I guessed. Nietzsche never grew such a moustache. These amounts of hair appeared on his upper lip only during his last ten years of life, during which he was helplessly insane. He was unable to care for himself, and this responsibility fell to his sister, who allowed the 'tache to flourish and brought people in to do portraits. Poor Freddy had no choice. This picture of an intense mad-eyed walrus is probably not how Nietzsche would have liked to have been remembered! His sister, who managed to distort his work as well as his image, has a lot to answer for.[3]

To return to Taoism... The Tao, usually translated as "way", is seen as that force which underpins, interpenetrates, and flows through the universe. Actually, "flows through" is misleading, as it conjures up images of 'things' as vessels through which the Tao passes. Taoism admits of no such duality. And the Tao's primary characteristic is that it cannot be defined. A definition of it, such as "the process of the universe", may loosen our categories a bit in order to contemplate it, but categories ultimately have to be destroyed if that process is to be fully apprehended. I think Nietzsche was too suspicious or ignorant of 'mysticism' to fully admit it, but I suspect any Superhuman state would involve a similar destruction—or transcendence—of categories.

3. Nietzsche did in fact cultivate quite a 'tache even as a young man. This detail is wrong, but the general point about the grim portraits of him during his catatonic years holds firm. [2007]

So what is this process, or Tao, that we're trying to apprehend? In Nietzsche's words, it is "that *which must overcome itself again and again*". Nietzsche's conception of embracing this, of fully participating in the process of life, is shot through with an distinct emphasis on struggle—assertion, strife and conflict. Regarding modern occultural misinterpretations again, it is primarily in this sense that he intended his many references to war. Being anti-state and anti-political, Nietzsche in no way 'advocated' bloody economic and territorial battles between nations. He didn't 'condemn' them either. Nietzsche was neither liberal nor fascist. He largely used the word "war" in the sense of resolutely striving for self-mastery without shrinking from—rather, embracing—the inevitable conflicts this quest entails. "I will not cease from Mental fight, Nor shall my Sword sleep in my hand..." (William Blake, *Milton*)

It took me a while to reconcile this relentless struggle, which is obviously part of the path to self-perfection, with the supposed passive quiescence of Taoism. In the end, of course, it's a false dichotomy, and Christopher S. Hyatt seems to have summed it up best in his book *The Tree of Lies*:

> *The concept of surrender has become so distorted that many believe that "surrendering" is in opposition to power, sex and self mastery. This is one of the greatest lies. ... self mastery is not possible without surrender. This issue cannot be overemphasized. Magic and Mysticism—The Will To Self Mastery and The Will To Surrender—are two sides of the same coin. ... when power or love are taken to their extreme they become one.*

The Tao is a struggle of perpetual self-overcoming—*again and again*. But as Alan Watts ceaselessly points out, it is a struggle devoid of 'anxiety loops'. In fully surrendering to the flow of life, one surrenders one's resistance to the rolling process of destruction and creation, 'war' and 'peace', that true life constitutes. Passivity is often part of this resistance, as much as frenetic anxiety can be.

Satanism and Taoism are alike in that they are both deeply concerned with the hard/soft, strong/weak distinctions. Satanism seems to emphasize and value 'strength', while Taoism seems to emphasize and value 'weakness'. I feel that both may learn from each other. Taoists who have made the clichéd image of the quiescent oriental sage their behavioural ideal would do well to meditate on the Tao at work in an ocean whipped up by a tumultuous thunderstorm, and see how close to 'nature' they really are. Hardened Satanists, intent on fortifying their unbending will, would do equally well to take a sword to a piece of solid wood, and then to a pond. The wood will splinter and be destroyed. The pond will passively accept the blade, and effortlessly flow back to perfection once it is withdrawn.

> *I was made with a heart of stone / To be broken with one hard blow / I've seen the ocean break on the shore / Come together with no harm done*

Perry Farrell, 'Oceansize'

Satan's Ancestry

> *Those who point the finger at Satan, reveal Satan. Those who fight Satan, give him power. Those who blame Satan, give him influence. Those who talk much of Satan, create him.*
>
> *But those who worship Satan, tame Satan. Those who passively resist him, earn his respect. Those who accept him, diminish his influence.*
>
> *And those who analyse him, learn his wisdom.*

Lionel B. Snell, 'The Satan Game'

THE CHRISTIAN DEVIL, Satan, is an archetype. Whether one sees archetypes as creations of the human mind, genetically-rooted universal 'templates' of conscious experience, or fully independent spiritual entities, is irrelevant here. Even if archetypes are seen to be autonomous 'beings'—gods, goddesses, demons or spirits—they are inevitably experienced by means of our own bodies and minds. Our experience of them is filtered through whatever biological, cultural and psychological structures we happen to find ourselves equipped with to make sense of the world. Thus, if we're talking about the realms of human experience (and what else can we talk about in a useful way?), Satan may be seen to have a history, a mythical family line of descent. Certain universal facts of life, such as the processes of sex, birth & death, will be ever-present in most mythical figures; but the specific figures themselves evolve throughout human history to mirror the complex cultural interactions and upheavals that have ceaselessly manifested since the first time apes developed language, culture and myth—and became human.

IN THIS SPECULATIVE Satanic genealogy we shall obviously work backwards, climbing down from contemporary branches, down the trunk, and under the ground where the roots lay hidden. So to begin with, how is Satan conceived in contemporary culture?

Modern Christianity has lost much of the medieval iconographic vividness in its conception of Satan, as it is supposedly more 'sophisticated', and not given to simplistic anthropomorphisms (i.e. Satan as a reptilian, horned, cunning and wily beast-man dwelling 'down there' in his burning lair). The most significant manifestation of modern Christians' concern with their Devil is in the phenomenon known as the 'Satanic Abuse Myth'. 'Satanic Abuse', because the phenomenon centres around the conviction that the Western world is infested with invisible networks of evil Satanists, who ritually abuse and bloodily sacrifice people—usually children—in the service of their Dark Lord. 'Myth', because this conviction has uniformly been found, by government-commissioned investigations and independent researchers alike, to be false. Certain cases of abuse have been found where the perpetrators used the paraphernalia of occultism to terrify their victims into submission and silence. But not one case of genuine Satanists, occultists, or pagans harming children for the purposes of magical ritual has ever been found. So we can see that these obscene Christian fantasies of blood-soaked orgies and child sacrifice are merely the modern version of the medieval equivalents, the witch-hunts (or of the Roman equivalent, where early Christians were accused of similar crimes…). The vividness of these modern scapegoating fantasies seems to have made the mythical figure of Satan himself less necessary. Who needs an image of a subterranean Devil on which to project your repressed fears and desires when you can conjure up such horrifying scenes of 'actual' human activity?

Often at the forefront of the cultural panic around Satanism was the self-styled leader of California's Church of Satan, Anton Szandor LaVey. He seemed amused as well as indignant about the latest bouts of witch-hunt scaremongering. He knew as well as any open-minded observer that more children have suffered abuse and molestation at the hands of trusted Christian priests than have even heard of the Church of Satan. And his codes of Satanic practice are there for all to read: "Do not harm little children. Do not kill non-human animals unless attacked or for your food." (from 'The Eleven Satanic Rules of the Earth')

But for Satanists as well as Christians the actual mythical image of the Devil has become less central. LaVey states that Satan is "a representational concept, accepted by each according to his or her needs." This seems mightily hazy without LaVey's repeated reminders that 'Satan' roughly translates from Hebrew as 'adversary' or 'opponent'. Satanism is based on the principle of opposition. This is usually seen as opposition to the *status quo*, specifically Christian morality. Satan is an emblematic concept presiding over the practice of all those wonderful un-Christian things: free sexuality, autonomy, indulgence, harmony with (instead of dominion over) nature, and anti-authoritarianism. Many Satanists seem to slip up on this last one, and it's here that most Satanism as it stands loses my sympathies. Just as many people forget that Nietzsche's 'destructive-creativity' is meant as a perpetual process, not just a one-off revolution, Satanism can often slip from being an expedient release from Christian programming into being a dogma in itself. It seems to find it hard to challenge itself as an institution. There are many parallels here with the 'left hand path' of politics, Marxism. Many unsophisticated Marxists still think that their beliefs could function wonderfully as they stand once capitalism is cast to the ground once and for all, not seeing that their present beliefs are conditioned by their capitalist context. If Western capitalism is ever 'overthrown', I think many Marxists will follow their historical predecessors and become the new despots, or just be at a loss as to what to do without 'the opposition'. Substitute 'Satanists' for 'Marxists', and 'Christianity' for 'capitalism', and you have a wildly simplistic, but very revealing analogy.

The influence of Chaos Magic[4] and all its kindred philosophies on modern occulture seems to be a useful counter to this tunnel vision of simple opposition. The heart of Chaos Magic is the practical implementation of Nietzsche's vision of life overcoming itself again and again, and provides a good antidote to any sliding towards dogma, or dependence on a static adversarial figure.

To RETURN TO SATAN, we can see that despite his modern transformations, the popular conception of the Devil still bears the unmistakable hallmarks of pre-industrial Christianity's vivid image of him. He is almost always bestial. The horns and the cloven hooves are synonymous with the Devil, and a reptilian tail is often attributed to him. Related to this is his unmistakably sexual nature, often seen as a threatening or perverse sexuality, but definitely sexual. The conception of Satan as the rebel angel Lucifer is a bit of an anomaly here, and this figure seems like a more refined, sublimated and 'humanized' Devil, all ferality turned into stubborn pride, and sinister sexuality emerging as cunning seductiveness.

Pre-twentieth century Satanism, exemplified by people like Phillipe the Duc D'Orleans and Sir Francis Dashwood, was the domain of rebellious and hedonic aristocrats. Their repudiation of the asceticism of Christianity often involved the kind of debauchery modern Christians are eager to pin on modern Satanists. There is evidence of child murder and ritual sacrifice. Many, however, penetrated beyond frenzied opposition to the Church and discovered the intimately related, but deeper roots of Satan in

---

4. A modern magical current that stresses a flexible approach, in which belief is seen as a multi-purpose tool rather than a monolithic "creed". [2007]

pre-Christian pagan gods. Bloody sacrifice was usually part of such old paganism, and we'll return to this later. For now it is sufficient to see that the figure of Satan cannot be separated from the nature gods of the older religions.

Modern Satanists are often quick to deny this connection as being necessary or significant, probably eager to hang on to Satan's supposed status as a god in his own right, independent of both Christianity and nature worship. I suppose they fear the potency of their god being quelled by his being subtly appropriated into the realm of 'neo-paganism', derided (in some cases accurately) by Satanists as wishy-washy. But the connections are there.

For a start, it's plain that the Christian Satan was evolved as part of the church's expansion into pagan or 'heathen' lands. This process was often complicated by unforeseen overlaps between Christianity and indigenous pagan practices, to a certain extent betraying *Christianity's* pagan origins. We see this clearly in Catholicized Central and South American countries, where many natives have blended the invading cosmology into their own. A vivid example of this is the fact that indigenous Mexican mushroom cults call their fungal sacrament *teonanácatl*, meaning 'flesh of the gods'. Those cults which survived the Spanish conquest could easily accept the god Jesus, who offers us his flesh to eat, and his mother Mary, who became the new bottle for the old wine of Earth-Mother goddess figures. Invading Christians spreading north over Europe consciously appropriated existing pagan festivals, and built their places of worship on ancient sacred sites to win over the populace. But they still needed to weed out the more overt paganisms. So the widespread Horned God or Goddess, who presided over pagan nature worship and fertility rites, was demonised. Through the installation of dualistic categories of good and evil, and the identification of pagan gods as evil, they gave themselves permission to trample paganism into the ground and a lot of spiritual clout with which to terrorize natives into obedience.

The greatest insights into Christianity and Satan can be gleaned from exploring the Greek god Dionysus. He is very typical of pagan nature gods: he is horned, signifying kinship with animals (like the closely related goat-god of the Arcadian pastures, Pan, another source of Satanic iconography); he is a 'dying-and-rising' god, reflecting the cyclic process of the seasons in nature; and he has a strong wild and untamed aspect, again like Pan, forming a bond with pre-civilised humanity. It's obvious how Satan, Christianity's repressed shadow, has derived from such an archetype. In its irrational suppression of sexuality, nature, cyclicity and the body, Christianity latched on to this archetype and pushed it so far away from human experience that it became alien, and we became alienated. The already feral, ego-shattering Dionysian godform became

Pan and Dionysus in the Greek National
Archaeological Museum, Athens

utterly evil and terrifying, a force to be held at bay at all costs.

Now things get confusing. Did not Jesus, like Dionysus, die and rise again? Both are intimately associated with vines and wine; both have been connected to the use of psychedelic mushrooms; the flesh of both is in some way eaten as part of their worshippers' rites; and both names, according to John M. Allegro's *The Sacred Mushroom and the Cross*, stem etymologically from the same Sumerian root. There's almost as much evidence connecting Dionysus with Jesus as there is with Satan.

It's my feeling that we have here a crucial fork in the history of archetypes. Christianity appropriated the more abstract spiritual motifs of dying-and-rising nature gods (mainly supposed 'life after death') and up popped the mythical Jesus. The chthonic associations with the Earth, with sexuality and the body, were all repressed, compressed and demonised into Satan. In this division was lost all cyclicity, all the transformative and change-affirming power of nature's process. We descended into truly profane time; linear time instead of rhythmic, spiralling, sacred time. Norman O. Brown has noted that "the divorce between soul and body [analogous to the Jesus/Satan split] takes the life out of the body, reducing the organism to a mechanism". Likewise, the conception of an extra-terrestrial, eternal time (Heaven) as sacred renders the Earth profane, and binds us to the linear track of uni-directional historical 'progress'. We may see ourselves as moving towards this sacred time—but it is an ever-receding carrot-on-a-stick, and tears us away from omni-directional immersion in the moment.

No eternal reward will forgive us now for wasting the dawn.

Jim Morrison

IN SATANISM, SATAN is seen as embodying the principle of division and duality, that principle without which manifestation—matter, flesh, bodies & sex—cannot occur. This is symbolized in the 'inverted' pentagram, where two points are directed upwards and one down. The dual realm of manifestation rules over the singular, united realm of spirit. In the 'normal' pentagram the spirit rules the flesh. Jesus is seen as opposing Satan, and embodies the spiritual principle of unity. So what are we to make of the actual historical beliefs and practices of the followers of these two figures? Christianity has turned out to be militantly dualistic, denying the body and ravaging the Earth, glorifying the 'spirit' and longing for some united heavenly kingdom. And Satanists, while obviously prioritising flesh over spirit, ego over collectivity, are inevitably involved in many practices which approach Dionysian revelry, serving to abolish individual distinction. Also, their emphasis on living for the moment instead of "spiritual pipe-dreams" could be seen to destroy the future-fixation of profane time, following Nietzsche into a whole-hearted immersion in the eternal present.

Our problems in analysing these contradictions betray our present evolutionary and cultural problems. In looking at the splitting of Dionysus, we're seeing the mythical reflections of a phase in the development of the human species where the increase of city-dwelling and changes in agriculture and economics began to erode our bond with the rest of the biosphere. City walls are the rigidification of human ego-barriers writ large. "When Christians first distinguished themselves from pagans, the word 'pagan' meant 'country-dweller'. For the first centres of Christianity in the Roman Empire were the great cities—Antioch, Corinth, Alexandria, and Rome itself." (Alan Watts, *Nature, Man & Woman*) In our quest to urbanize our existence, to become as independent as possible from the less comfortable and benign aspects of nature, we have become lost in a mire of confusion. Witness Blake's disgust at the industrial revolution in his phrase "dark Satanic Mills", and the fact that most of the mill owners were probably devout Christians. Protestantism has been intimately linked to the rise of capitalism by psychoanalytical historians; Satanists advocate material power. A church in Coventry recently held a service in thanks for the car industry; and Jesus advocated shunning possessions and said rich people would have a bloody hard time getting into heaven. Such confusion seems to be the price for living under the sway of false dichotomies like Jesus/Satan, spirit/matter, collective/individual, intellect/instinct.

Culture and civilization are inseparable from material technologies, and things are no less confused in the technophile/Luddite debate. The real dichotomy to be tackled here is that of harmonious/unharmonious technology. Do our tools help us achieve our desires, or do they *become* our desires? Do you browse the web to kill time and boredom, like TV, or use it to help you do what you want to do in the real world? Is our technology harmonious with nature? In most cases today, the answer is a painful *no*. We have lost the vision of the first grand tool-using age of humanity, the Neolithic, where culture, agriculture and technology were used to work with and *intensify* the natural environment.

Reclamation

OUR SATANIC GENEALOGY has so far reached the figure of Dionysus, and if we delve further back, we find *his* roots in the pan-European Neolithic worship of the Great Goddess. In Greek myth, Dionysus' mother is identified as Semele, a mortal. She was, however, sometimes equated with Ge, the Thracian form of the Earth Goddess Gaia.

> *The male god, the primeval Dionysus, is saturated with a meaning closely related to that of the Great Goddess in her aspect of the Virgin Nature Goddess and Vegetation Goddess. All are gods of nature's life cycle, concerned with the problem of death and regeneration, and all were worshipped as symbols of exuberant life.*
>
> Marija Gimbutas, *The Goddesses and Gods of Old Europe*

Now I shall lose the interest of yet more die-hard Satanists. I think it's possible to trace most of Satan's aspects and characteristics back to the Neolithic (and perhaps Palaeolithic) Great Goddess. It's true that if you gathered all available books on Goddess worship together, the vast majority of them—in their style, typography, illustrations and attitude—would probably be… well, *twee*. It's obvious why the figure of the Goddess is largely consigned to the realm of New Age Pap; but I think a serious, unromantic investigation of the religious and mythical complex termed 'the Goddess' will uncover something a lot more challenging, vital and *useful* than the trite New Age-isms we're usually presented with.

The Neolithic Goddess, like Satan, was invariably **horned**; the ox was one of her most revered forms. Being associated with the Earth itself she was often a chthonic (underworld) Goddess, this aspect entering Greek mythology in the story of Demeter and Persephone. It's worth noting that Heraclitus once said that Dionysus was another name for Hades, lord of the underworld. The whole chthonic goddess & son complex is the basis for our image of Satan ruling over a subterranean Hell.

> This horned aspect is thought by some researchers to derive from the 'horns' of the womb, the Fallopian tubes—the form of which can potentially be proprio-cepted, or felt internally, in states of heightened consciousness.

Another strong link between the Goddess and Satan is the serpent. The serpent in Genesis' Garden of Eden is often associated with Satan, and Christianity usually extends this association to all snakes. The snake was, along with the ox, the animal most frequently associated with the Neolithic Goddess. The spiral, often symbolizing a coiled serpent, is one of the most common Goddess symbols. Archaic serpent myths from around the world are far too numerous to detail here. However, one extremely early myth (perhaps the earliest), which detours us to an extremely bizarre connection with Christianity, is well worth going into.

In his book *Blood Relations*, anthropologist Chris Knight proposes that human culture was the result of early female *Homo sapiens* synchronizing their menstrual cycles. This collectivity, he argues, empowered them to periodically 'sex strike' during menstruation—females basically refused sex with their partners (but possibly had menstrual sex with male kin) until the men went hunting and brought back enough meat to feed them and their children.

The full thesis is persuasive but very complex. It is enough for now to note that the hypothesized collective act of female synchrony was achieved through tidal and lunar observances, utilizing these natural, universal cycles with which widespread groups of women could 'phase-lock' and harmonize their own blood cycles. In the Australian Aboriginal myths of the Rainbow Snake, and its associations with menstruation, water, the moon and women, there is widespread acknowledgement that this 'cosmic serpent' (often androgynous) originally gave women *power*. Knight's key argument is that this power is the power to periodically unite in saying 'no' to sex, to initiate sexual-political change (the Snake symbolizes the united body of 'flowing' women). At the same time, it is the powers of **shamanism and magic**, which Knight sees as evolving as a result of the first 'proto-cultural' groups of humans in Africa dispersing inland, away from their coastal origins. The females, robbed of the tide as one of their main cyclic guides, evolved moon-scheduled ritual activities—and thus symbolic culture—to synchronize social, psychic and bodily rhythms.

> "The link of blood and magick can also be found in the German word for 'sorceror', which is 'zauberer'. The word goes back to OHG *Zaubar*, MD *Tover*, OE *Teâfor* ... All three words mean 'red colour, red ochre, to colour in red'!" (Jan Fries, *Helrunar*)

Somewhere along the line, as the myths and practices of many surviving hunter-gatherer tribes testify, this power was appropriated by men. Knight sees male initiation ceremonies involving cutting the penis or arm (found among Australian Aborigines and other indigenous cultures), together with the existence of extreme menstrual taboos, as evidence for a male take-over of female ritual power. One male Aborigine, speaking of their all-male rituals, told C.H. Berndt that "all the Dreaming business came out of women—everything; only men take 'picture' for that Julunggul [i.e. men make an artificial reproduction of the Snake]. In the beginning we had nothing; because men had been doing nothing; we took these things from women." The surviving Snake myths, propagated by all-male initiation societies, portray the Snake as threatening to women. Part of this threat is derived from myths that describe the Snake swallowing women; Knight feels that this once symbolized the power of synchronized menstruation to unite women, together 'in the belly of the Snake'. Male initiation societies utilizing the Snake mythology may see this devouring serpent as somewhat threatening, but still desire the womb-return, unity and rebirth of being swallowed. Much as Jonah is willingly cast into the sea to be swallowed, then vomited out by the "great fish" prepared for him by the Lord God.

Knight finds hard evidence of similar 'Rainbow Snake' myths across Africa and South America, all closely related to tides, rain, floods, menstruation and lunar cycles. The myths perpetuate these associations, but are often configured to make women see the Snake as a threat. There are some tribes, however, whose women still draw power

Hercules and the Lernean Hydra

from the Snake, and celebrate it in menstrual rites. Knight also interprets the myriad 'dragon' (i.e. mythical serpent-beast) legends as remnants of this archaic mythical conception of women's culture-forming menstrual synchrony, and of the male take-over. Many dragon myths speak of many-headed beasts (the Hydra for instance), and this is possibly an echo of the menstrual Snake which comprised many women in unison. Of course the classic dragon tale, across the world, says that valiant men *rescue maidens* from its clutches, *destroy* it, and gain *power*. Given Knight's

theories, there could be no clearer mythical equivalent of a male usurpation of female power: overcoming a reptilian representation of their blood-unity and menstrual ritual potency.

Now, let's have a look at the Holy Bible. Turn to Revelations 12:

And there appeared a great wonder in heaven; a woman clothed with the sun, and the moon under her feet, and upon her head a crown of twelve stars:

And she being with child cried, travailing in birth, and pained to be delivered.

And there appeared another great wonder in heaven; and behold a great red dragon, having seven heads and ten horns, and seven crowns upon his heads. And his tail drew the third part of the stars of heaven: and the dragon stood before the woman which was ready to be delivered, for to devour her child as soon as it was born. ... [She gives birth to a sort of second Christ, and flees into the wilderness. Michael casts the dragon out of heaven. The dragon persecutes the woman, who is given eagle wings to escape.]

And the serpent cast out of his mouth water as a flood after the woman, that he might cause her to be carried away by the flood. [Aboriginal Rainbow Snake myths are connected with great floods in Australia's past.]

Very strange to find such a twisted distortion of what may be a primal human myth of *the beginning* (of culture) in the ravings of a religious visionary supposedly being granted a glimpse of *the end*. This vision corresponds in some way to the frequent 'male-appropriation' myths of modern hunter-gatherers: in depicting the dragon/serpent as threatening to a woman; and in the statement that the denizens of heaven "overcame him by the blood of the Lamb" (12:11). The Lamb is Christ, and Christ is a man who bled from his arms (and, like all Jewish men, he presumably bled from his genitals, when he was circumcised as a child). Interestingly, one New Age commentator on Revelations believes that because the many-headed dragon "has several autonomous decision-making centers, [it] is therefore the very epitome of disorganization, of centrifugal or dispersive forces." (F. Aster Barnwell, *Meditations on the Apocalypse*) Think back to what Knight believes the original Rainbow Serpent represents, and compare.

And who was this blood-red, water-spewing, many-headed dragon? Saint John the Divine tells us that he was "that old serpent, called the Devil, and Satan...". A day or so after making this Rainbow Snake-Dragon-Satan link, I started reading *The Wise Wound* by Penelope Shuttle and Peter Redgrove. They take a Jungian approach to the few systematic instances of menstruating women's dreams being recorded. Apparently, some women's dreams at this time contain strong male figures, often threatening or sinister. Shuttle & Redgrove's idea is that menstruation can be a time of heightened sexuality and departure from conventions for women, hence its widespread repression and extreme taboo status. They see the appearance of a compelling male figure in menstrual dreams as the appearance of the *animus*, a Jungian word for the masculine principle in women. Talking about the repression of menstruation leading to a "negative animus", they say: "If the woman's menstruation is despised, that is, a deep instinctual process in her is ignored or hated, then its spirit will return with all the evolutionary power of those instinctual processes that grew us and continue to energize our physical being. You could say in this way that the Christian Devil was a representation of the animus of the menstruating woman, in so far as the Christian ethic has Satanized woman and her natural powers."

I WANT TO FOLLOW these Goddess/Serpent/Devil associations now by focusing on one specific place (which will also lead us to other areas I'm interested in): Avebury in Wiltshire, with its rich psychogeography and densely inter-related complex of Neolithic monuments.

Michael Dames has analysed the Avebury monuments, synthesizing archaeology, folklore & ethnography, to build a vision of a harmonious cycle of structures embedded in the local geography. They form a ritual landscape which reflects the cyclic narrative of the seasons and of human life. The monuments are seen to celebrate and embody the Great Goddess, conceived in the pervasive form of the Triple Goddess: Maiden, Mother & Crone. (Being three multiplied by itself, the number nine is frequently given a high status in Goddess-based religions. It seems no coincidence that modern Satanism has adopted this as its central number.)

The massive Avebury henge is approached from the south and west by two long, slightly winding stone avenues. Dames' contention is that these two avenues are processional serpentine pathways by which young men and women approached the henge for marriage and consummation ceremonies. The men's Beckhampton avenue, to the west, is largely destroyed. It seems significant, though, that the name Beckhampton derives from the Old English word meaning 'back'. Dames relates this to the spine, and to Tantric beliefs in the raising of the Kundalini serpent energy from the base of the spine.

Much more evidence survives in relation to the partly intact West Kennet avenue, beginning at the Sanctuary (the name for the remains of a circular wooden temple at the southern foot of Waden Hill). Comparisons with contemporary Neolithic symbolism and ethnographic studies show that the Sanctuary (corresponding to the springtime Maiden) was probably a site for the initiation of young girls reaching puberty. This conjecture, along with the proposed serpentine nature of the processional avenue leading to consummation in the henge, is supported by Chris Knight's research. Aboriginal mythology equates the Rainbow Snake with the ritual dance through which women collectively synchronize their menstrual periods (or with which men are united in blood-letting initiatory rituals). As the onset of a girl's puberty is signalled by

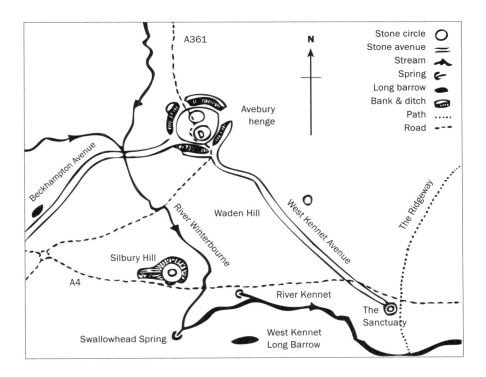

their first menstruation, Dames' theories about the function of the Sanctuary and the symbolic serpentine nature of the West Kennet avenue stand on quite firm mythical ground.

At the henge, the male and female snake-avenues conjoin. Dames argues that the so-called 'D' feature within the southernmost of the two stone circles inside the henge is a representation of the tip of the phallic Beckhampton avenue snake entering the henge. This is 'swallowed' by the females' West Kennet snake, whose gaping jaws may be seen to be symbolized by the southeast and southwest quadrants of the henge, the actual stones representing its teeth. The dual sexual symbolism of the serpent—penetrator and devourer—is not lost on Dames. He speaks of the Beckhampton avenue's "commitment to bisexuality" as it approaches ritual sexual union in the henge; we'll return to his androgynous Avebury Goddess later.

The vast stone standing at the point where the West Kennet avenue joins the henge is commonly known as the Devil's Chair. Also in the Avebury area we have the Devil's Den long barrow; and there are too many caverns and Neolithic standing stones in the

British Isles named after the Devil to catalogue here. The demonisation of indigenous paganism that was such an integral part of Christianity's conquest of these islands is prolifically demonstrated in such folkloric names.

In 634 CE a Christian church was built up against the west bank of the Avebury henge. On its twelfth-century font is depicted a bishop, armed with a spiked crozier and a Bible, fending off two serpentine dragons. However, the battle waged against the powerful chthonic forces of nature glorified in the Avebury monuments wasn't some abstract war of symbols. In the fourteenth century most of the stones in the southwest quadrant of the henge were destroyed by Christian authorities trying to eradicate the many "superstitions and questionable practices" still connected with the stones.

In Dames' ritual landscape cycle we move from the henge southwards to the awe-inspiring Silbury Hill, a flat-topped conical mound of earth which stands as the largest man-made Neolithic structure in Europe. Known to have been built progressively over many years, added to each August (harvest time), it seems likely that this was the Neolithics' vision of the pregnant Earth Goddess made flesh. Natural breast- and belly-like hills and mounds were commonly worshipped in many archaic cultures, but the emergence of agriculture signified the rising importance in human *participation* in nature. Silbury Hill—the Mother Goddess labouring to give birth to the year's crops—is a monumental testament to a culture whose technology still harmonized with nature, working mythically and practically at precisely the same time.

Excavations have revealed that at the core of Silbury lies a circular wattle fence and stacked layers of turf forming an inner mound. The wattle fence has exactly the same diameter as the Sanctuary, and most projected reconstructions of the wooden temple at the Sanctuary reveal it to be identical in size and form to the inner Silbury mound. Silbury, then, is a fractal reflection of the Sanctuary, which is replicated within and then magnified eight times in the total mass of the Silbury mound. The springtime Maiden has matured into the life-giving Mother of the harvest. A careful study of Dames' investigations into the harmonic fractal resonances within the Avebury complex (all monuments being based around natural units of measurement taken from the springs feeding into the revered River Kennet) is capable of pushing the rational mind beyond itself into a deep, awe-full respect for the powerful visionary precision of this 'primitive' culture.

Of course, being the most provocatively sensuous and voluptuous of all the Avebury monuments (go there!), Silbury failed to escape the demonisation of Christian folklore. There is a legend that the Devil was once on his way to attack Marlborough (just east of Avebury) by dumping an apron, or spade full of dirt on the town. The bishop of

Silbury Hill

Marlborough apparently stopped him at the last minute; the Devil dropped his load, and Silbury Hill was formed.

The last monument in the cycle, before it completes a total gyration and feeds back into itself at the Sanctuary, is the West Kennet long barrow. It is located just southeast from Silbury and almost due east from the Sanctuary. This multiple burial chamber is the Goddess in winter: the Crone, the death-dealing Dark Goddess found (and so often repressed) in many religions. The barrow is constructed—like other European Neolithic burial chambers—to render yet another form of the Goddess' body. You go in through her stone vulva, and enter a small corridor with five small adjoining womb-tomb chambers.

Despite its belief that faith in the Lord Jesus Christ will automatically transport his followers to an eternal realm of happiness, love & old friends on dying, Christianity is terrified of death. Most systems of belief promoting a simplistic, personal and linear form of immortality are—they deny death. "Hell, Luther said, is not a place, but is the experience of death, and Luther's devil is ultimately personified death." (Norman O. Brown, *Life Against Death*) Again we see that Christianity has ruptured, repressed & demonised the cyclic processes of nature. To cultures harmonized with the seasonal rounds, death precedes life just as death follows life. The Avebury cycle, where each distinct monument participates in the unified ritual landscape, suggests a culture where the principle of division has not yet been separated from the principle of unity; death is part of life.

The barrow was built around 3250 BCE, and remained open until around 2600 BCE, when a huge stone forecourt was erected, and the chambers were packed with a mass of chalk rubble, organic material, and bits of bone and pottery (resembling the chalk, soil and vegetable layering found in the core of Silbury, whose foundations are contemporary to the sealing of the barrow). During its 'active' time, the barrow was almost certainly used for ritual as well as burial purposes. Dames points out that "the belief that the living can find meaning and reality within putrefying chaos was once widespread", and rightly notes the possible parallels with Tantric practices.

The loving Goddess of Creation has another face. As she brings man into time and his world, she also removes him from it. So she is his destroyer as well. No-one can be a successful Tantrika unless he has faced up to this reality, and assimilated it into his image of the nature of the Goddess. There are many rituals, some of them sexual, carried out among the corpses

Christianity, especially in rural areas with a deep pagan tradition, can never entirely purge itself of the past. In the parish church of Ilkley, West Yorkshire, there is a stone carving which is usually identified as the Romano-British goddess Verbeia (below). In her hands she holds two writhing snakes, resembling the famous Minoan snake goddess statuette found in Knossos, Crete. Verbeia is said to be goddess of the River Wharfe, which flows through Ilkley, forming the familiar goddess-serpent-water associations. However, one historian of Ilkley believes the goddess is only superficially associated with the river itself, and was once associated with the brooks flowing down from springs on the famous neighbouring moorlands. On these moors are numerous prehistoric rock carvings, stone circles, and traces of human settlement dating back to 7000 BCE; Verbeia is probably a survival of more ancient myths in the area. The historian notes the double snake symbol's connection with healing (look at the British Medical Association's symbol), and the long-standing reputation of the moor's waters for healing properties, which survived into Victorian times, when a renowned healing spa was set up near the edge of the moor.

in real (or symbolic) cremation-grounds, which bring this necessity forcibly home to the practising Tantrika. There, in the red light of funeral pyres, as jackals and crows scatter and crunch the bones, he confronts the dissolution of all he holds dear in life.

Philip Rawson, *Tantra: The Indian Cult of Ecstasy*

We can never know the exact nature of the rites enacted in the West Kennet long barrow, but many of the skulls and thigh bones from the dead buried there were found to be absent. The obvious explanation for this is that they were used in Neolithic rituals, probably at the nearby causewayed camp on Windmill Hill, northwest from the henge, where many individual skulls were found. Dames notes that "the widespread use of skull and femur in fertility rites was maintained down to classical times, when the rotting flesh fell off to reveal the clean tools of a new sexuality, with skull acting as female container, encompassing the thigh bone-phallus." I'm also reminded of the use of skulls and thigh bones in various 'left-hand path' (i.e. frowned upon) cultic practices in Tibet. It's clear that any study of Neolithic Goddess-orientated cultures will fruitfully profit from comparisons with non-mainstream Asian religious beliefs.

"Although there is very little information concerning the megalithic monuments of the West, Hindu texts contain the entire ritual for setting them up, and for the orientation of sanctuaries, etc. All studies on European prehistoric religions should thus be based on the Indian documents available." (Alain Daniélou, *Gods of Love and Ecstasy*)

The Snake Goddess

A FEW YEARS AGO, shortly after I had become interested in paganism, but well before I began any of the above research, I had a very bizarre dream. I dreamt I was an actor in the process of making a film whose director was a very sinister and shadowy figure. There was an unnerving atmosphere on the set, and I kept finding small, partially hidden pentagrams and other similar symbols—sewn into the undersides of cushions and so on. I became convinced that the script and set were devised so that the specific motions and gestures the unwitting cast made during filming would have the equivalent effect of a ritual to evoke the Devil. In the half-dream hypnopompic state before fully waking up, I had the distinct sensation of physical pressure around my anus. Dream logic convinced me that this was in fact Satan. I was vaguely disturbed during the following day, but the dream quickly faded into the past.

Earlier this year, I was writing something about the idea that dreams and vision states are in fact the perceptual flip-side to interior bodily sensations. The two realms can be seen as two different 'channels of perception' conveying information about the **interior processes** of the human organism, from visceral energy streams to the sub-molecular goings-on in the brain. Going to sleep one night, having just finished the section on this particular subject, I had a hypnagogic experience that seemed to confirm my theory, and shed revealing light on the dream of the Devil a couple of years before.

I was in a pretty low state, and half-heartedly (pathetically actually) called on the Earth Goddess to visit me in my dreams that night. Soon after, I found myself getting up from the bed and walking across my room. I was suddenly overpowered by incredibly intense body sensations, and felt my mind 'blacking out' as if I was fainting. I instinctively 'knew' that this was the power of the Goddess overtaking me, and tried hard to surrender to it as I fell down ('trying hard' in these situations is a classic mistake!). I found myself lying on the floor, a huge lump obscuring my vision in my right eye. I heard the woman who lives across the hall from me trying to get in. My fall must have been *loud*, I thought. I took the lump on the right side of my face to be a result of the fall, and desperately tried to work out how I could get up to open the door and let the woman in. I couldn't move, and feared that I'd really injured myself. At the same time I became aware of rattling noises in my kitchen. There was a distinctly female presence in there. Then I snapped out of it—I had been half-dreaming. I was still in my bed, and the 'lump' was a bit of the duvet against my face. I instantly connected the two instances of female presence, one seemingly trying to help me, with my vague plea to the Goddess.

Suddenly, immense surges of energy began to flow around my body, intense and strangely familiar streamings that pushed me into a delicious and frighteningly precarious balance between waking and dreaming. Then I *felt* pressure around my anus… and what followed can only really be described as being fucked by the, or at least a Goddess. A stupendous thrust of energy rushed up me, and I was immediately propelled into a highly vivid and intense lucid dream. I was flying high above a scintillatingly real landscape, a deep blue summer sky above me, a daytime sky yet dotted with stars. Part of the subsequent dream involved fishing a demonic-looking pike out of a lake—this

> In *The Wise Wound*, Shuttle & Redgrove investigate the possibility that menstrual cycles have the potential to be affected by lunar cycles in that the pineal gland, which may also affect sexual development, can sense subliminal changes in light. Noting its traditional association with the 'third eye' of inner visions, they speculate that "Just as our visible eyes obtain visual information from the outer world, so does our invisible third eye, the pineal, convert into visual images experiences from within the body. This argument is supported by painstaking evidence."

seemed to be the culmination of a series of intense dreams I had recently had about seeing fish swimming underwater. The pike, once on land, turned into a cute brown seal.

I awoke from the dream after escaping from a very nasty situation by flying straight up through the building I was in, bursting through each floor successively and waking with a jolt on blasting out the top. It didn't take much meditating on all the sensations and symbols to realize I had almost certainly just experienced a bizarre manifestation of the Kundalini serpent energy.

THE KUNDALINI SERPENT is envisioned in traditional Tantric yoga as being a coiled-up (spiral) reservoir of normally untapped psychosomatic energy, stored in the *Muladhara*, or base chakra. The base chakra is located in the perineum, just in front of the anus. Kundalini is a goddess at the same time as being a spiral snake energy. Kundalini Shakti is the female principle to Shiva's male principle in Tantra's erotic cosmology. The goal of Tantric practice is to awaken the dormant snake Goddess through various yogic methods, causing her to surge up the body and ecstatically unite with Shiva at the highest chakra. This rising can be seen clearly at either end of my dream (and body)—both in the energy thrust up me from my perineum just before sleeping, and in the climactic flight through the floors of a building, eventually out of the top, into waking consciousness.

> Tantrism holds that the deities presiding over the base chakra are Brahman and Dakini—who is the red, menstruating goddess.

Many insights (and a tremendous feeling of well-being) flooded through as a result of my Kundalini dream. Firstly, there was the gnostic confirmation of my theories about Satan being (for me at least) a demonised remnant of a primal serpentine Goddess. My dream of a few years ago was undoubtedly the same Kundalini phenomenon, distorted by the Christian cosmology virus, and undeveloped. It seemed to be a 'confirmation', rather than being an experience *induced* by my research, because the Kundalini dream reflected so precisely back onto a dream I had long before any of my research began. And at the time of the second dream, although I had been looking into Goddess myths, I had not really looked at Kundalini. The fish symbolism seemed to flesh out my feeling that the Kundalini phenomenon is the prime model for looking at this experience. In Indian mythology, the fish symbolizes Kundalini's most primitive form. Interestingly, early Christians represented Jesus (eternal opponent of the serpent Satan) with a fish symbol. Jesus opposes fish to serpents in Matthew 7:10—perhaps yet another example of divisive Christian mythologizing.

Kundalini has been connected by Gene Kieffer (a president of the Kundalini Research Institute in New York) to the UFO contact experience, after personal psychic activity that involved both phenomena. This connection, and the sensations I experienced of pressure around the anus (or nearby perineum), inevitably brought to mind the infamous reports from supposed UFO 'abductees', who believe themselves to have been improperly probed up the arse by bug-eyed scientists from other planets. Are we looking here at spontaneous Kundalini vision states, either distorted through confusion or overlaid with a space-age clinical myth-structure?

My current belief that visions and the body's energy processes are complementary has given me a rough rule of thumb in understanding my-

> The !Kung, a southern African tribe, describe their entry into trance (which they call *!kia*) in a way that strongly reflects Kundalini experiences. They believe that a primal supernatural potency, *n/um*, resides in the pit of the stomach or the base of the spine. Frenetic dancing causes the *n/um* to 'boil', and it ascends the body until it peaks in or near the skull—inducing full *!kia*, and initiating shamanic soul-flight. It is interesting that the social and ritual life of the !Kung has retained one of the most vivid emphases on menstrual puberty rites known. Also, they believe that the power of *n/um* is most efficiently transferred via the sense of smell. In Tantra, the Muladhara chakra is associated with this sense.

thology: *all the most resonant and meaningful myths will reflect some aspect of biology and evolution.* As Shuttle and Redgrove say in *The Wise Wound*, "mythology and physiology are only two sides of the same thing, which is alive." Of course, evolutionary theory and the physical sciences can be seen as yet another myth-structure; and seen in this way they should, if they are to relate to the general human experience of life, somehow echo the more primeval and recurrent mythologies and archetypes of our cultural ancestry. The idea that the Kundalini serpent, which ascends the spinal column, is the psychosomatic evolutionary force in the human body, can be seen to relate to the fact that we are vertebrates. Our common evolutionary inheritance, along with all mammals, birds, reptiles, amphibians and fishes, is that we have a backbone. We have all physically relived the evolutionary journey of bodily mutation as we gestated in our mother's wombs. Human embryos, in their earliest stages of development, are successively indistinguishable from fish, reptile, bird and other mammal embryos—at one stage, recognizable gills emerge, and then atrophy.[5]

Our individual lives begin in the amniotic ocean of the womb. Organic life on Earth began in the oceans. And humanity itself may have emerged from a partial

5. Ernst Haeckel's theory that "ontogeny recapitulates phlyogeny". The 'strong', literalist version of his theory is now widely discredited, though I feel the idea still expresses a more general truth. [2007]

return to the ocean. Many anthropologists believe that humans evolved on the shores of east Africa, as hominid apes returned to a semi-aquatic lifestyle. This is seen to account for our hairless bodies, the layer of buoyant fat beneath our skin, and possibly our upright posture (a distinct advantage if you're trying to keep breathing whilst wading through deep waters).[6]

It seems quite fitting that Indian mythology should symbolize evolutionary power through the snake, the skeleton of which is basically a backbone, and the fish, the original spine, which still inhabits life's womb.

ANY FORM OF ANAL STIMULATION contains the possibility of ecstatic spiritual experience. Phil Hine has pointed out that Ramakrishna experienced Samadhi whilst having a dump on more than one occasion, and this is interesting in relation to Martin Luther's so-called *Thurmerlebnis* ("experience in the tower"), a revelation about faith that was to inaugurate Protestant theology. The 'tower' was where the toilet was located in Luther's Wittenburg monastery. "This knowledge the Holy Spirit gave me on the privy in the tower." (Luther) In his analysis of Protestantism in *Life Against Death*, Norman Brown hones in on the centrality of the Devil to Luther's theology, and on the 'anality' of the Devil. He documents Luther's numerous associations of the Devil with 'filth', 'blackness' and foul odours, and notes his methods of counter-attack to the Devil's assaults—at one revealing point he threatens to "throw him into my anus, where he belongs." These scraps of information, the traditional location of the base chakra, and my intuition that Satan may be related back through history to a primeval serpent goddess, seem to be no coincidence.

"In the human body, the strait gate leading to the earth-centre, or snake goddess, is the anus." (Alain Daniélou, *Gods of Love and Ecstasy*)

Many traditions, from male Aboriginal initiation ceremonies to Aleister Crowley's magick, recognize the power of sodomy to elicit altered states of consciousness, but this is mostly ignored in our own culture due to the extreme taboo associated with anal eroticism (and with altered states themselves). This taboo is clear in homophobia, but is equally present in heterosexuality. Often, sodomy is not merely tabooed, but actually illegal—such is the continuing power of old Judeo-Christian restrictions over modern secular prohibitions. Perhaps (as far as our own culture is concerned) the strength of the taboo against sodomy, and not necessarily the physical act in itself, accounts for its potential to induce powerful spiritual experiences.

6. See *The Aquatic Ape Hypothesis* by Elaine Morgan. [2007]

Spirituality is, at heart, a breakthrough into a wider realm of consciousness, and is thus frequently associated (as in Tantra, Chaos Magic and Satanism) with breaking the conventions and laws that inevitably shape consciousness. The danger here, as ever, is that of becoming obsessed with the breaking of a single restriction. Once a restriction is overcome, new and different restrictions may fall into place. For instance, a Satanist who has endeavoured to break the traditional Christian taboo against rational self-interest and ego-gratification may find him or herself liberated in many ways. Eventually, though, this process of liberation may restrict that person from expressing spontaneous selflessness. The path of liberation has no end.

Sodomy, then, may well be a powerful step on the path of spiritual and sexual liberation, but rigid correlations and associations may eventually become obstacles. Regarding the association of the base chakra with the anus, Phil Hine has cautioned against the idea that chakras, or energy centres, have literal physical locations: "I'm working on a body-alchemy centred approach to the chakras at the moment, and the muladhra, for me, relates to one's physical sensation of the here & now. A great deal is made of the muladhra being the 'seat' of Kundalini-shakti—but again, too many people have interpreted Kundalini stuff in terms of getting away from the body, towards some kind of rarified 'spiritual' state. My own feeling is that the Tantric perspective is less about 'awakening kundalini' as though it were something static, and more about 'becoming aware' of kundalini's living presence in, and around us. This necessitates, of course, a change in how we perceive ourselves, and the world we are enmeshed in." (personal correspondence) Hine's first 'Kundalini' experience involved an influx of energy coming *down* his body. This 'contradiction' of the traditional experience can also be seen in Reichian therapy. Wilhelm Reich's theory of bodily 'armour' (rigidified musculature, seen to be arranged in sections like the head, throat, chest, etc.) corresponds well with the chakra system. But in opposition to the yogic assertion that one must work from the bottom up when opening the chakras, Reich advised therapists to work from the top down in undoing armour.

So, anal eroticism is merely one of many gateways to sexual and spiritual ecstasy. And while individual proclivities and specific cultural circumstances channel erotic bodily energy through particular pathways, any broad overview must take into account a holistic view of the body. The many 'maps' of the body, from the chakra system to Freud's anal, oral and genital organizations of sexual energy, are all ultimately limited. The least limited map of bodily energy, the map under which all others may be subsumed, is that described by Freud as 'polymorphous perversity' and by mystics as 'oceanic consciousness'. It is the chaotic, spontaneously self-organizing state a baby experiences before the narrower maps of its culture impose themselves on its body—and which anyone may experience in ecstatic release from cultural boundaries.

In *Love's Body*, Norman Brown has pointed out that the human body, in its deepest levels, is not as linear and static as our culture's vision of it suggests. There is a profound interconnectedness and interpenetration at work. The main component of our linear vision of the body is the divided polarity of the head and the groin, the brain and the genitals. But… "The word cerebral is from the same root as Ceres, goddess of cereals, of growth and fertility; the same root as *cresco*, to grow, and *creo*, to create. [Richard] Onians, archaeologist of language, who uncovers lost worlds of meaning, buried meanings, has dug up a prehistoric image of the body, according to which the head and genital intercommunicate via the spinal column: the gray matter of the brain, the spinal marrow, and the seminal fluid are all one identical substance, on tap in the genital and stored in the head." An aspect of this ancient model can be seen to derive from agricultural fertility symbolism. In corn, the seed is literally in the head of the plant.

Further, echoing our discussion of Kundalini, Brown remarks: "The classic psychoanalytical equation, head = genital. Displacement is not simply from below upwards; nor does the truth lie in simply reducing it all downwards (psychoanalytical reductionism). The way up is the way down; what psychoanalysis has discovered is that there is both a genitalization of the head and a cerebralization of the genital. The shape of the physical body is a mystery, the inner dynamical shape, the real centers of energy and their interrelation…" The 'genital organization' of sexuality, where the genitals are the prime channel for sexual energy, is seen by both Freud and Reich as the 'healthy', 'normal' mode of eroticism in humans. Neither could conceive of a culture that could withstand the dissolution of this pattern and support groups of polymorphous humans, people for whom sexuality pervades their entire body, and thus their whole lives. Evidently we're still a long way off from such a culture, but it seems important to recognize that anything less is a limitation of our potential for generating, using and exchanging energies. Brown's refutation of purely genital sexuality applies equally to all forms of restricted eroticism or spirituality:

> *Erect is the shape of the genitally organized body; the body crucified, the body dead or asleep; the stiff. The shape of the body awake, the shape of the resurrected body, is not vertical but perverse and polymorphous; not a straight line but a circle; in which the Sanctuary is in the Circumference, and every Minute Particular is Holy…*

The Androgyne

MOST STRIKING, PERHAPS, is the sexual ambiguity of the goddess in my dream. She was definitely a feminine presence, yet the rising snake-energy nature of her conjunction with my body put her in the cock-bearing masculine role. This perception was given a bit of consensus validation when I visited a friend in Brighton, who I hadn't related my dream experience to. He was skimming through another piece I wrote relating to the World Tree being seen as the spine up which the Kundalini serpent rises. Out of the blue, he said, "Oh yeah! I had a Kundalini thing once when I was tripping, lying on the ground at a festival. It was like being fucked by Mother Earth." (I had related the Kundalini goddess to the Earth goddess myself—I had an strange experience of energy rushing up into me from the ground at a Dreadzone gig months before my dream. Also, the base chakra, where the Kundalini serpent is traditionally seen to be coiled and dormant, is connected in the chakra system to the earth element.) On the same journey, I visited a friend who I did tell my dream to. He quickly related it to an experience he had had while on mushrooms next to a vast boulder in the place where the sarsens (local sandstones) used to build the Avebury henge were taken from. He experienced it as a bolt of energy penetrating him from below, and nicely called it "an amphetamine pessary up the psychic jaxxee."

The Goddess is an hermaphrodite.

> *In Neolithic thought, maleness was an aspect of the universal being, or vessel, which was regarded as female. How could it be otherwise, if she truly encompassed everything? An architectural expression of this view is often found in Indian temples, where the overall form displays the feminine creative shape, based on the womb cell which contains the Lingam or male element.*
>
> Michael Dames, *The Avebury Cycle*

On Windmill Hill near Avebury, the oldest structure to be found is a cluster of 32 pits dug around 3700 BCE. Dames points out that this pit grouping can be seen to form the outline of a goddess figure, squatting with upturned arms in the traditional stylization of a woman in labour. The pit corresponding to the vulva is "the largest and most fully furnished of all the pits", containing pottery, worked flint flakes, hammerstones, and sarsen balls similar to others found beneath Silbury. However, if one does take the formation to be a squatting goddess, two of the central pits clearly form a penis shape. A small chalk slab, known as the Windmill Hill amulet, found in an adjacent ditch, bears a design similar to the pit goddess, and also displays lines apparently describing a phallus. Hermaphroditic motifs can be seen in two other carved chalk figurines found on the hill, and Dames also notes an androgynous Neolithic figurine found in Somerset and a Bronze Age goddess figure with a beard which was found in Denmark.

The heretical Knights Templar reputedly worshipped a 'demon' named Baphomet, most famously depicted by Eliphas Lévi as a goat-headed half-human deity, clearly male and yet breasted—with two intertwining snakes rising from his lap (an important image in Tantra). Baphomet was naturally taken by the Church to be Satan. The Templars were accused of Devil worship and sodomy, and in the early fourteenth century King Philip IV of France had 54 of them arrested, tortured and killed on

heresy charges. Satan himself sometimes has shades of androgyny. Phil Hine has informed me that Robertson Davies, in his collection of short stories *High Spirits*, holds Satan to be an hermaphrodite. And the figure of the Devil in a seventeenth century drawing called *Witchcraft*, by Claude-François Ménestrier, clearly has big dangling breasts.

Baphomet by Eliphas Lévi

Dionysus, familiar to us here as precursor of the Jesus/Satan split and son of the Earth, was raised by women, often jeered at for his effeminate appearance, and referred to by a king in a text by Aeschylus as "man-woman". Alain Daniélou presents copious documentation, in his book *Gods of Love and Ecstasy*, that Dionysus is almost precisely equivalent to the Indian god Shiva—from whom we may also derive another traditional aspect of Satan, the trident, which is closely associated with Shiva. One of Shiva's principal aspects is the *Ardhanarâshvara*, the hermaphrodite. "The Prime Cause may be conceived as masculine or feminine, as a god or a goddess, but in both cases it is an androgynous or transexual being."

In Siberian shamanism, as in many shamanic traditions, ritual bisexuality is held to be a sign of sacred power, of dealings with other worlds.

Witchcraft by Claude-François Ménestrier

Daniélou also notes that the Etruscan prophetess wore a phallus attached to her girdle. **Kucumatz**, the supreme god of the Quiché Indians, is androgynous, both father and mother of all creation. Jewish mysticism elaborates on the creation myth of Genesis in the idea of the primordial androgynous being, Adam Kadmon, a perfect reflection of the divine (see Genesis 1:27—"So God created man in his own image, in the image of God created he him; male and female created he them."). S/He is split into Adam and Eve to form humans.

Androgynous figures in mythology represent a state of diversity-in-unity and unity-in-diversity that transcends the apparent opposition of sexes and genders. They are vivid, bodily images of a recurrent spiritual impulse to unite, but not leave behind the

Kucumatz is equivalent to the Mayan resurrection god Kuculcan and the Aztec culture-hero, moon-god and creator of humanity, Queztalcoatl (both these names mean 'feathered serpent'). Hunbatz Men, a modern Mayan daykeeper and ceremonial leader, has attempted to reconstruct the initiatory sciences of the ancient Maya in his book *Secrets of Mayan Science/Religion*. In analysing etymology and surviving Mayan temples, he concludes that the Mayan religion was based around a system of seven energy centres, very similar to the Hindu chakras. In both systems, the realization of a divine serpent-power is the goal. In Tantra, it is Kundalini. In Mayan tradition, the serpent is Kuculcan, but there is also the Mayan word *k'ultanlilni*—built up from *k'u* ('sacred'), *k'ul* ('coccyx', the base of the spine), *tan* ('place'), *lil* ('vibration'), and *ni* ('nose'). This amalgamated word embodies the Mayan equivalent of a yogic tradition. Men also discusses a seven-headed serpent form carved on a monolith in Aparicio, Veracruz, Mexico (right), and notes that the Buddha was bitten by a seven-headed serpent while in the river of initiation. "This serpent is called chapat in India. Curiously, the people of the Yucatan, Mexico have the same word and it, too, refers to the seven-headed serpent, just as in India."

ecstatic interplay of opposites—without which unity would be a bland mess, with no contrasts, dynamism or fun. This impulse can be seen more abstractly in the Taoist yin-yang symbol, and the *coincidentia oppositorum*, or union of opposites, in medieval alchemy. Referring to androgynous motifs in mythology, Mircea Éliade says that this "nostalgia for primordial completeness ... is found almost everywhere in the archaic world."

So what does this mean for us? A recognition that, potentially at least, gender is less a barrier than a permeable membrane (to paraphrase Carol J. Clover in *Men, Women*

& *Chainsaws*), and that this membrane may be a gateway to magical consciousness. Whatever the sexual orientation involved, truly ecstatic sex (ritualized or not) can lead to a psychic intertwining and transmutation of sexual identities. Even in (or maybe especially in) the exploration of the *extremities* of sexual difference, this potential may emerge. As Chris Hyatt says, opposites taken to their extremes become one. Or—as in the yin-yang symbol, where at the extreme of dark yin we find light yang emerging, and vice versa—the **opposites become each other**.

I once went to a talk by two practising process-oriented psychotherapists (therapy based on the work of Arnold Mindell), and the woman there responded to a question about Freud by deriding his 'oppressive' theory of 'penis-envy', the idea that women are screwed up because they haven't got that all-important cock. Later in the talk she got round to talking about sexual experimentation, and expressed tingling excitement about the possibilities raised by strap-on dildos. Now, I think Freud *was* pretty ridiculous in a lot of his thinking—but not always because he was

> "If no attempt is made to induce the orgasm by bodily motion, the interpenetration of the sexual centres becomes a channel of the most vivid psychic interchange. While neither partner is working to make anything happen, both surrender themselves completely to whatever the process itself may feel like doing. The sense of identity with the other becomes peculiarly intense, though it is rather as if a new identity were formed between them with a life of its own." (Alan Watts, *Nature, Man & Woman*)

necessarily *wrong*, just distorted and one-sided. The pendulum's swung right across to the other side in many feminist circles, where 'penis-envy' is refuted because it's 'oppressive', and then men's 'womb-envy' or 'menstrual-envy' is given as an explanation for why men are all screwed up.

Hang on! Learn from the androgyne. Maybe both these 'envies' exist. And maybe we can ditch that word 'envy', and all its associations with eternal frustration. Both Freud and the fundamentalist feminists base their theories on the supposedly unchangeable biological foundation of our sex. But these immutable biological 'envy' theories just seem to me to be signs of a lack of imagination. Change 'envy' to 'desire' and cross-dressing or role-playing may be sufficient to transcend biology, for a time, with enough imaginative energy. Strap-on dildos for women and arses in men need a little less imagination. Still further, there are the presently available surgical techniques of transexualism. And if the permanence of this step scares you off, perhaps soon the intelligent and creative application of new technologies, such as virtual reality or nanotech biomechanics, could offer us unlimited exploration of our inherent sexual plasticity and mutability.

Flesh

It is evident that certain rites and practices of ancient Shivaism or Dionysism, such as human sacrifices, could not be contemplated nowadays. Perhaps I should have avoided mentioning them, as they could easily be used as a pretext for rejecting the whole of Shivaite concepts, but, in my opinion, it was necessary to do so because they reflect tendencies of the human being and aspects of the nature of the world, which it would be imprudent to ignore. They form part of our collective unconscious and risk being manifested in perverse ways if we are afraid to face up to them.

Alain Daniélou, *The Gods of Love and Ecstasy*

GOING RIGHT BACK to where we started, let's recall that the primary manifestation of the modern Church's concern with the Devil is its fantasy of rampaging Satanists or pagans sacrificing animals and children to the Dark Lord. Modern human sacrifice is largely a **myth**; however, I see no reason for doubting that animal sacrifices occur, though not necessarily just by 'Satanists' (note Anton LaVey's 10th Satanic Rule: "Do not kill non-human animals unless attacked or for your food."). Almost all religions have a deep, intrinsic history of animal sacrifice, and some still practice it. The Massai of Kenya and Tanzania, though nominally Christian, continue to practice blood sacrifice. So do followers of Santeria, a combination of African religion and Christian symbolism, in the States. They regularly ignore U.S. laws (which prohibit the killing of animals except in licensed butcheries and for animal experimentation) in order to practice their religion. The chief contemporary practitioners of ritual sacrifice seem to be Christians themselves, who slaughter and eat tens of millions of turkeys every year as part of their celebrations of the birth of their god.

> This myth is cleverly played upon in the early seventies horror film *The Wicker Man*, which on the surface seems to be a standard cash-in on these lingering suspicions about paganism. However, the way the Christian copper (who is eventually burnt) is lured into the trap is revealing. It's only because he's so repressed and suspicious of pagans that he falls for the bait. He comes to the island and is convinced that a 'missing' girl is going to be sacrificed—what else would these phallus-worshipping heathens who cavort naked around bonfires be up to? All the 'evidence' turns out to be carefully contrived to play upon his rampant Christian suspicions: the girl is part of the plot, he is trapped by his own projected fears, and sacrificed in a ritual for crop success. If this was real life, of course, all the islanders should be up on conspiracy to murder. As the piece of art that it is, the story works perfectly as a delicious example of poetic justice.

Human sacrifice also has a long history. It seems to be the main element of Neolithic Goddess cultures that most modern popularisers of Goddess religions have neglected to deal with. Joseph Campbell has said that "human sacrifice is everywhere characteristic of the worship of the Goddess in the Neolithic sphere"; Avebury is no exception. Dames details many instances of human sacrifice in Neolithic Avebury: a prehistoric urn full of human bones was found in the southern inner stone circle of the henge; an adolescent male was found in the foetal position, with all bones broken, within the Sanctuary; other young men have been found buried along the West Kennet avenue. One was found with a thigh-bone jammed into his jaw—sexual/fertility symbolism which involves these sacrifices in one of the primary concerns of the Avebury monuments, the success of the crops. Dames speculates that the sacrificial victims could have actually been honoured to play this part: "For the victims, the opportunity to end their lives in physical incorporation with the Great Serpent [the West Kennet avenue] may have been regarded as an awesome privilege, an ultimate union with the godhead—son and parent united in divinity." The overwhelming holism of the surviving monuments seems to suggest that life for these people may well have been so unified, and death so deeply intertwined with life in their psyches, that young men could have felt their death to be a privilege, an opportunity to spill their life-blood into the ground and magically give life to the crops and the community—as well as return to the womb of the Earth-Mother.

The idea of sacrifice, bloody or not, is at the heart of human religious life. Its basis is surely the food chain—the interdependence of all life on all other life, the fact that nothing lives save by another's death. Alain Daniélou has called blood sacrifice "the sacralization of the alimentary function", that is, the ritualisation of killing and eating. "The whole universe is really only food and eater." (*Brihat Aranyaka Upanishad*) "The world as sacrifice; this world as food; to be is to be eaten." (Norman O. Brown, *Love's Body*) If the world is conceived of as one divine body, the process of life is divine autophagy—self-eating. It seems that all religious sacrifices may be derived from the recognition of this fact. Most practices are distorted to a greater or lesser degree, but the original function of sacrifice was probably part of the human urge to *intensify* the processes of nature. Vegetarianism and veganism do not negate the fact that life thrives on death—only an unholistic, anti-animist view of life would hold that plants are not living creatures like the rest of us. And while modern technology makes vegetarianism viable for us all (and meat-eating cruel, relying as it does on modern techniques of slaughter), the symbolism of sacrifice and blood are rooted in the consumption of animal flesh.

What do we actually mean by 'sacrifice'? The dictionary definition is "the act of giving up something valued for the sake of something else more important or worthy." Alan Watts says that it is an act which makes something holy (*sacer-facere*), arguing that "sacrifice is only accidentally associated with the cessation, death or mutilation of the offering because it was once supposed that, say, burning bulls on an altar was the only way of transporting them to heaven." (*Nature, Man & Woman*) This idea is used to stress that 'sacrificing' one's sexuality to God does not mean chastity, because if you're not fucking, there's nothing there to 'sacrifice', or 'make holy'.

These two definitions, 'giving up' and 'making holy', seem to be at odds—you can't make your cake holy and eat it—until we look at Shivaite (Shiva-worshipping) practices that forbid anyone to eat any flesh that is not the result of a ritual sacrifice. "One should not eat the flesh of living beings without killing them oneself, i.e., taking a conscious part in their slaughter and making the gods a party to it, since the world which they have created and uphold is itself a perpetual sacrifice." (Daniélou) In a system where "the gods must be offered the first-fruits of the harvest, the first mouthful of all nourishment", this practice makes an offering—gives something up—as well as making the act 'holy'. In killing for food in the name of Shiva, the sacrifice forms a ritual intensification of nature, of divine autophagy. As in Dionysian rites, the animal is seen as a manifestation of the god, with whom the worshipper communes through the act of eating. You are what you eat. The pagan origins of the Christian communion should be plain. "Eating is the form of redemption. Except ye eat the flesh of the Son of man, and drink his blood, ye have no life in you." (Brown)

The practice of Shivaites, of only eating what you yourself ritually kill, seems diametrically opposed to the systems of hunting and eating taboos anthropologists have discovered among hunter-gatherers. Chris Knight postulates a primitive 'own-kill' rule: "Culture starts not only with the incest taboo, but also with its economic counterpart in the form of a rule prohibiting hunters from eating their own kills." One's 'own blood', in both senses of blood lineage and totem animal blood, is forbidden. This 'rule', he argues, is demonstrated by the fact that their exist so many methods of getting around it. Rules are there to be broken; their boundaries, and thus the rules themselves, are defined by how they are circumscribed. The ways of getting around this rule can be seen in its application only to a man's 'first kill'; in tribes where you can eat your own kill provided you apologize to the animal's spirit; and in customs where you symbolically offer your kill to someone else first, whether it's another person or a god. Knight sees the latter as the basis of most 'sacrifice'.

His reason for postulating this 'rule' is that his model of the origins of human culture sees the first proto-human apes involved in an evolving system of menstrual, sexual, hunting and economic taboos. We looked earlier at how Knight envisions culture as emerging from women synchronizing their menstrual periods. Tied up to this is the idea that the time of menstruation, the dark moon, would be immediately followed by hunting trips, as the moon waxed. Because proto-human females were more burdened by their offspring (human infants take a lot longer to mature), they needed to secure a sure supply of food for themselves and their young. In short, they needed to make damn sure the males didn't go off hunting, scoff the lot while they're away, and only come back with scraps (as often happens in groups of apes). Knight believes that part of the women's menstrual 'sex-strike' (against procreative, 'domestic' sex at least) involved a growing system of associations between menstrual blood and the blood of game animals. The taboo against 'domestic' sex during menstruation would be psychically linked to a taboo against eating raw, bloody flesh. In Knight's model, the women control the fire hearth, and thus it is only through presenting their kills to the women that the men can have cooked flesh, free of the tabooed blood. This way, food for the women and children is assured. Survivals of this taboo system are found in most contemporary hunter-gatherer tribes. To take one example, hunters of the Urubu tribe in the Amazonian basin may not bring deer into the village. The hunter deposits his kill at the edge of the clearing, and sends a woman to get it. The Urubu believe that "a hunter who brought his own game into the village would be punished with a terrible fever and become *kaù*, crazy." Californian Indians even have a special verb, *pi'xwaq*, which means "to get sick from eating one's own killing".

Knight's model is interesting in that so many ecstatic nature-based religious cults *directly* contravene these postulated 'primeval taboos'. "Ancient Shivaite or Dionysiac ritual does not allow the cooking of the flesh of the animal victim, which had to be captured after a chase, torn apart and eaten raw." (Daniélou) If prohibitions against eating raw meat form part of the basis of human culture, these later ritual practices may be seen as *counter-cultural* forces. They evolved during times when human life was beginning to be urbanized, and 'culture' was becoming something very alienated from nature. Shivaism and Dionysism stand against conventional civilization, and aim to ecstatically commune with the natural forces and spirits of the land.

Humans irrevocably evolved into cultural beings in eastern Africa long ago. Some development beyond animal existence was obviously necessary for 'culture' to exist at all; thus the raw/cooked, nature/culture, animal/human oppositions. But when the rural/urban opposition arose, as the great cities of Eurasia formed, something was slowly lost. Evolution was turned back on itself as human culture, a profound outgrowth of nature, began to isolate and alienate itself from its source. "The Dionysiac rite takes its followers back to a primitive stage, which is the antithesis of the city cults in which the victim is eaten cooked. Here we find a very ancient contrast between the two concepts of food and its associated rites. When Dionysus is himself the victim of the Titans who put him to death and boil and roast him, his being cooked implies that Dionysus, as the god of Nature, is the victim of the gods of the city." (Daniélou)

THE MENSTRUAL BLOOD and animal blood connection also reveals the second source of sacrificial blood symbolism: menses, the blood which women shed every month as part of their bodily fertility cycles. This may be the original 'human sacrifice', in that menstruating women 'give up' their womb-lining and their unfertilised egg.

> *It is possible that shamanistic practises of possession by articulate and helpful spirits originally came from the upsurge of energies at the period. There are indications that these spirits were sometimes seen not only as animals, but as the spirits of unborn children. That is, the blood of the period would come instead of the pregnancy, and the blood spoke with the spirit of the unconceived child. A distressing development of this would be in the rumoured cults where children were aborted for magical purposes: there would be no need for this in a menstrual cult where the natural energies were listened to by women aware of their existence.*
>
> Penelope Shuttle & Peter Redgrove, *The Wise Wound*

Throughout history, many diverse groups have been accused of child murder or ritual abortion: Dionysian cults, medieval witches, early Christians, Jews in Nazi Germany, Satanists (and non-Satanic pagans) in the modern West. The widespread repression of menstrual power seems to be a good explanation for the projected fantasies that such accusations usually are.

Throughout Aboriginal Australia, there is no other way to arouse the Rainbow Snake than by bleeding, whether this is menstrual blood or the blood of men who cut themselves. The Snake is summoned by and attracted to blood. Perhaps this archaic myth-logic is the origin of the reasoning behind the modern occult theory of blood. Talking of *larvæ*, or elemental spirits, Eliphas Lévi, a nineteenth century French occultist, says that "such *larvæ* have an aërial body formed from the vapour of blood, for which reason they are attracted towards spilt blood ["hence come the histories of vampires", he says later] and in the older days drew nourishment from the smoke of sacrifices." In connection with this, he notes that "according to Paracelsus, the blood lost at certain regular periods by the female sex and the nocturnal emissions to which male celibates are subject in dream people the air with phantoms." (Note that Paracelsus includes semen along with menses—both are in some sense 'unborn children', and both are highly valued in most sex-magic traditions.) Blood is seen in such occult theory to contain the 'life-force' of the organism, and spilling the blood is thought to release this energy—usually to 'feed' a god or spirit, so that it can be manifested, or empowered to do the sorcerer's bidding. Such sacrifice is part of many voodoo traditions.

Christopher Hyatt and Jason Black, in *Pacts with the Devil*, concisely reveal the modern double standards surrounding the issue of animal sacrifice.

> *Recently, on a national new broadcast, there was a segment taped in New York. The video showed ranks of cages containing sheep and chickens, with NYPD officers standing with military solemnity in front of them. The police, the commentator informed us, had just "rescued" these animals. Not from torture or some other form of lingering abuse, but from a place where a major Santeria festival was about to be celebrated. What was to be the fate of these livestock animals? They would be killed expertly and quickly by a Santero, the blood given to the Orishas as a gift, and most likely (depending on the ritual) the animals would be cooked and eaten that same evening by the men, women and children at the celebration.*

They point out that we live in a society where someone could be sat at home eating a steak (from an animal cruelly, sometimes slowly killed in a slaughterhouse), spy someone living next door swiftly killing a chicken as part of a ritual, and run terrified to the phone to inform the police about this 'Satanist', even if the ritualist ate the chicken later for dinner. Who is more humane? Hyatt & Black also note that all 'kosher' meat, drained of blood while a rabbi says a blessing, is by definition ritual sacrifice; yet this is legal. Now, I'm wholly and unreservedly against any animal being killed if it isn't eaten (unless in self-defence). When it is eaten, I think this falls into the category of personal choice. It's not my business if people want to eat animals without cruelty. Likewise, it's not my business if they want to use the animal's death for spiritual purposes before they eat it. Or if they want to kill it cleanly, then rip it to shreds and eat it raw with their bare hands.

What Hyatt & Black show is the hypocrisy surrounding blood sacrifice in modern culture. I wonder how many fundamentalist Christians involved in spreading the anti-pagan 'ritual sacrifice' scam sit down at Christmas and happily chew the cooked flesh of poultry kept in appalling conditions and slaughtered profanely. Given the choice,

I would rather the turkey's death formed part of a Santerian ritual, and its flesh eaten afterwards by people fully conscious of its demise—and of the sacredness of life and death.

Blood

WHEN I FIRST READ the evidence for the 'own-kill' taboo in hunter-gatherer tribes—which in some extreme cases extends to hunters believing that even having *seen their food alive* would lead to bad hunting luck—I thought immediately of the modern meat industry. Now we haven't the *slightest* chance of seeing the creature we're eating in its living state. But this modern taboo merely serves to isolate meat-eaters from the reality of death (as one would expect in a Christianity-based culture). For hunter-gatherers, who still kill, even though they may not eat their own kills, the reasons are a bit more complicated, and a little less alienating.

As a general example of how the own-kill rule functions in hunter-gatherer societies, let's look at what is commonly known as 'totemism'. Say there are several clans of hunter-gatherers living in the same area. Each clan has a 'totem animal'. For simplicity's sake, let's say that there's the bear clan and the deer clan. Now, the own-kill taboo would work here by preventing the bear clan from eating bear flesh and the deer clan from eating deer flesh. Each clan would be responsible for the *hunting and killing* of their own totem animal, and for supplying the meat to the *other* clan. The own-kill rule therefore functions as part of a reciprocal gift-giving system of exchange. Such exchange systems form part of the basis for human culture and language. Sharing and swapping necessitates communication and agreed-upon behavioural guidelines; and the evolution of such guidelines and communication likewise facilitate more intricate systems of exchange. There is strong evidence that most hunter-gatherers link (or rather *identify*) this food taboo/exchange system—of which there are countless variations—with incest taboos. Thus, the Arapesh of Papua New Guinea equate the taboo against eating one's own kill with the taboo against incest. When asked about incest by an anthropologist, a man from the Arapesh tribe said, "No, we don't sleep with our sisters. We give our sisters to other men and other men give us their sisters."

Not all hunter-gatherer exchange systems are based on inter-tribal marrying that is so male-dominated, as many early anthropologists tried to claim (to vindicate current patriarchy). But whoever controls inter-marrying between tribes, matrilineal kin and totem animals are equated as being tabooed for a very simple reason: *they are one's own blood.* "To speak of someone as 'my own flesh' means, in many languages of the world, that the person is a close relative, usually by 'blood'." (Knight) To many tribes, whose word for 'flesh' is often the same or similar to their word for 'kin', this is more than a figure of speech. Malinowski, speaking of the Trobriand islanders, observed that when men learn that a sister has given birth, they rejoice, "for their bodies become stronger when one of their sisters or nieces has plenty of children." Likewise, a similarly concrete feeling of bodily connectedness is expressed by the Buandik of Australia when talking of totemic animals. When forced by hunger to eat such an animal, "he expresses sorrow for having to eat his *Wingong* (friend), or *Tumung* (flesh). When using the latter word, the Buandik touch their breasts to indicate close relationship, meaning almost part of themselves."

> *In fact, the evidence suggests a cross-cultural pattern in which totemic food avoidances [and incest taboos] are in some sense avoidances of the self. If one's 'taboo' or 'totem' is not one's 'meat' or 'blood' or 'flesh' in the most literal sense, it is at least one's 'spirit', 'substance' or 'essence'. And the crucial point is that the 'self', however conceived, is not to be appropriated by the self. It is for others to enjoy.*
>
> Chris Knight, *Blood Relations*

'Avoidance of the self' shouldn't be taken in the modern sense, like 'running away from yourself'. Implied here is an avoidance of the *isolated ego*. The hunter-gatherers' gift-giving and exchange systems imply a commitment to extending the **unity** an individual feels between hirself and hir clan or totem animal. This unity is felt so strongly that it need not 'feed on itself' to bind itself together—it can (and must) be shared with others. It *spills over*, forming reciprocal inter-tribal bonds of interchange.

Looking back to Shivaite ritual sacrifice, the eating of one's own kill could be seen as an attempt to regain some personal identity in societies where individuality is suppressed and compromised not to maintain kinship and transcend-

"Union and unification is of bodies, not souls. The erotic sense of reality unmasks the soul, the personality, the ego; because soul, personality and ego are what distinguish and separate us; they make us individuals, arrived at by dividing till you can divide no more—atoms. But psychic individuals, separate, unfissionable on the inside, impenetrable on the outside, are, like physical atoms, an illusion; in the twentieth century, in this age of fission, we can split the individual even as we can split the atom. Souls, personalities, and egos are masks, spectres, concealing our unity as body. For it as one biological species that mankind is one—the 'species essence' that Karl Marx looked for; so that to become conscious of ourselves as body is to become conscious of mankind as one." (Norman O. Brown, *Love's Body*)

ent blood-unity, but to support an oppressive and unhealthy social structure. However, since the whole point of Shivaism is to transcend the individual, and commune with nature, perhaps new psychic structures are involved. As I said before, Shivaism is *counter-cultural*. Maybe as the original cultural systems became corrupted in crowded cities, the only tack available to oppose this corruption was to oppose the principles it was based on—however socially useful and healthy they may have been in the past.

I haven't come across any information about sacrificial practices among hunter-gatherer tribes who practice the own-kill rule, and see common blood as the great unifier. But the whole idea of feeling yourself to be one with animals and other people—in a very tangible way—seems to me to have a strong bearing on blood sacrifice. Sacrifice, in the sense of "giving up something valued", would be truest if one lived with this feeling. Offering the blood (as life-force) of an animal to a spirit would mean much less if the animal involved wasn't felt to be part of one's own body. If this feeling was present and real, the sacrifice would truly be a sacrifice.

Following this logic, why bother with animals or other humans at all?

And as Deities demand sacrifice, one of men, another of cattle, a third of doves, let these sacrifices be replaced by the true sacrifices in thine own heart. Yet if thou must symbolize them outwardly for the hardness of thine heart, let thine own blood and no other's, be spilt before that altar.

Aleister Crowley, Liber Astarte vel Berylli

Crowley made exceptions to this 'rule' (as he had only one real rule, the often misunderstood "Do What Thou Wilt"); but the concept presented here—spilling one's own blood as a sacrifice—has interesting resonances. It echoes the idea expressed earlier that menstruation may be the original 'human sacrifice'. Chris Knight sees the emergence of all-male initiatory societies, involving self-mutilation and the spilling of blood, as a usurpation of female menstrual ritual power and solidarity. While we should obviously endeavour to release menstruation from the repression it has suffered—and all the evidence points to it being the most repressed and stigmatized human bodily function in history—the practice of ritual blood-letting in men today need not carry any of the associations with stealing women's power that it may have had in the past. I can imagine many a strident feminist deriding men cutting themselves as suffering from 'menstrual envy'. Well, we've already looked at this—I wouldn't consider it 'envy' so much as a *desire* to partake of the other sex. It is some sort to equivalent of women gaining erotic pleasure and insight through using strap-ons.

It seems that the aboriginal populations who travelled across the Bering Straits from Siberia—those who were to become the native peoples of the Americas—developed the sacrifice of ritual blood-letting further. In his essay, 'A Fashion for Ecstasy: Ancient Maya Body Modifications', Wes Christensen details Mayan practices of tattooing, piercing, and blood self-sacrifice. As well as men mutilating their genitals, the piercing of the tongue was common, in men and in women. As Christensen says, "The psychological equation of the penis and the tongue needs little reiteration." His view is that the practice of "pulling spiny cords through holes in the tongue" may have been important for female Mayan ritualists: "If the wounding of the Male expresses the desire to own the magically fertile menstrual flow by mimicking it, the symbol seems less important than its function of linking the opposing forces of mother/father, sky/earth in one ritual practitioner. This way of looking at the rite is less male dominated, as well, as it allows for the pervasive influence of women in the ritual life of shamanistic village life. The tongue sacrifice, then, is the woman sorcerer's rite—a rite in which she symbolically imitates the male to achieve the same equilibrium."

Genesis P-Orridge, who was involved in quite extreme spontaneous self-mutilation as part of his performance art activities in the seventies, has been performing rituals for nearly twenty years, and claims that he never does one without cutting his skin. "I have to make at least one cut on myself, and it has to be a cut that will scar, no matter how small." (*Re/Search: Modern Primitives*) Obviously, scarification requires care, precision, and knowledge of how different parts of the body will react to incisions. But it could form part of the prime effort underlying all mysticism: *overcoming subject/object dualism*. Alan Watts has described this in terms of the idea, or feeling, that one is an individual ego contained in a "bag of skin". 'I' (the subject) am inside, and you and everything else ('not-I', the object) are outside. The *skin* is seen as the limit-point between these realms. Most people would see this as 'common sense'. However, as Watts stresses, the skin is as much a bridge as a barrier. Many different forms of energy and matter—sweat, heat, sound vibrations—constantly cross this bridge, though we are usually unaware of it. We are inextricably bound up with the 'outside' world, to such an extent that we cannot exist without it. 'Out there' thus forms part of our identity, and our true body is the entire universe. "Originally the ego includes everything, later it detaches from itself the external world. The ego-feeling we are aware of now is thus only a shrunken vestige of a far more extensive feeling—a feeling which embraced the universe and expressed an inseparable connection of the ego with the external world." (Freud, *Civilization and its Discontents*)

> "Staring open-eyed at the blazing sun, the blinding rays burning deep into your skull, filling it with unbearable brightness... Blowing on an eagle-bone whistle clenched between your teeth until its shrill sound becomes the only sound in the world... Dancing, dancing, dancing from morning to night without food or water until you are close to dropping in a dead faint... Pulling, pulling away at a rawhide thong which is fastened to a skewer embedded deeply in your flesh, until your skin stretches and rips apart as you finally break free with blood streaming down your chest... This is what some of us must endure in the sun dance.
>
> Many people do not understand why we do this. They call the sun dance barbarous, savage, a bloody superstition. The way I look at it our body is the only thing which truly belongs to us. What we Indians give of our flesh, our bodies, we are giving of the only thing which is ours alone... It is only our own flesh which is a real sacrifice—a real giving of ourselves. How can we give anything less?
>
> Some white men shudder when I tell them these things. Yet the idea of enduring pain so that others may live should not strike you as strange. Do you not in your churches pray to one who is "pierced", nailed to a cross for the sake of his people? No Indian ever called a white man uncivilized for his beliefs and forbade him to worship as he pleased. The difference between the white man and us is this: You believe in the redeeming powers of suffering, if this suffering was done by somebody else, far away, two thousand years ago. We believe that it is up to every one of us to help each other, even through the pain of our bodies. Pain to us is not "abstract", but very real. We do not lay this burden onto our god, nor do we want to miss being face to face with the spirit power. It is when we are fasting on the hilltop, or tearing our flesh at the sun dance, that we experience the sudden insight, come closest to the mind of the Great Spirit. Insight does not come cheaply, and we want no angel or saint to gain it for us and give it to us secondhand." (John (Fire) Lame Deer, *Lame Deer: Seeker of Visions*)

And yet the illusion of the skin as an impassable physical and psychic barrier persists. Thus, cutting the skin could be a very powerful way of shattering this illusion. Scarification can be a form of ego-dissolution. For a start, pain is an intense physical stimulus, and can serve to heighten consciousness. Spiritual practices such as flagellation, bodily restriction, ritual scarification and piercing amply testify to the potency of pain as an intoxicant. In the practice of self-scarification, this alteration of consciousness could shift one's perception of the wound from being some 'symbolic' link between the inner and outer realms to being the concrete link which both physics and primitive tribes insist that it is.

Further, this theory opens up an understanding of many bizarre and perverse phenomena in human behaviour. Schizophrenics frequently lacerate their skin, something usually associated with mere self-destructive tendencies. But if we see this as self-destructive in terms of an attempt to overcome the illusion of separate individual existence (the isolated self, or ego), the practice of spontaneous self-mutilation can be seen as part of the healing process that many radical psychiatrists claim schizophrenia actually is. The 'split' in schizophrenia isn't the popular caricature of 'split personality' (which is found in multiple personality disorders), but the split between inner and outer, the retreat of the individual from the outside world. My own view is that this split is not an aberration found only in the 'mentally ill', but the standard psychic stance of 'normal' modern humans. Ego-dissolving catalysts like intense sex and psychedelic drugs wouldn't be subject to the repression that they are in our culture if this wasn't the case. Schizophrenia is thus the shock and confusion of spontaneous liberation from our aberrant 'normality', a descent into the depths of the psyche, an intensification of the inner/outer split through which one discovers the illusory nature of this division.

It is not schizophrenia but normality that is split-minded; in schizophrenia the false boundaries are disintegrating. ... Schizophrenics are suffering from the truth. ... Schizophrenic thought is "adualistic"; lack of ego-boundaries makes it impossible to set limits to the process of identification with the environment. The schizophrenic world is one of mystical participation; an "indescribable extension of inner sense"; "uncanny feelings of reference"; occult psychosomatic influences and powers; currents of electricity, or sexual attraction—action at a distance. ...

Dionysus, the mad god, breaks down the boundaries; releases the prisoners; abolishes repression; and abolishes the principium individuationis, substituting for it the unity of man and the unity of man with nature. In this age of schizophrenia, with the atom, the individual self, the boundaries disintegrating, there is, for those who would save our souls, the ego-psychologists, "the Problem of Identity." But the breakdown is to be made into a breakthrough; as Conrad said, in the destructive element immerse. The soul that we can call our own is not a real one. The solution to the problem of identity is, get lost. Or, as it says in the New Testament: "He that findeth his own psyche shall lose it, and he that loseth his psyche for my sake shall find it."

Norman O. Brown, *Love's Body*

The Divine Body

'THE GODDESS', like all forms of deity, seems to me to be much more than the 'personification' of natural forces, or aspects of ourselves. As the previous discussion of personality and ego-consciousness shows, this is because my conception of a 'person' or 'individual' is, at root, gradually evolving beyond the atomistic and divisive conceptions I have been indoctrinated with. Our conception of divine *personifications* will (or should) change along with changes in our conception of *personality*. Since we can't safely shift overnight to a chaotic, flux-based state of being, the traditional view of deities will still persist to an extent, as useful focuses for attention and energy; but just as any sexual channels must be subsumed under a broader polymorphic map, lest we become obsessed with any one channel, our relationship to 'deities' should be encompassed by a much wider conception of divinity. My brief teenage flirtation with Christianity collapsed mostly because I found the mental idea of God as an old bloke with a beard in the sky hard to get round—and very, very silly. I don't intend to let my present relationship with the Goddess fall prey to similar abstractions. Indeed, the foundation of my interest in this area is the shattering of abstract, monolithic, otherworldly conceptions of divinity.

MUCH AS MY IDEAS are preoccupied with balance, my present conviction that our 'physical' experience is the basis of all 'mythology' automatically places a distinct difference, an imbalance in emphasis, between those first two all-powerful beings we encounter—our parents. The physical root of my being is the fusion of a part of my mother with a part of my father, but this explosive cellular union is followed by nine months of incredibly rapid growth and development as part of my mother's body. Even after physical separation occurred at birth, my mother was probably more or less my 'world' for the first months of life, depending on circumstances. Freudianism seems to be right in saying that the primal shock of existence is separation from the mother, first physically and then psychically. I've no idea why this is the way things are, but such is the case, and I usually point this out to anyone whose knee jerks in dismissal as a reaction against the idea that the first human conceptions of divinity were female. Now, I think this view is overly simplistic, and should be tempered by the above discussions about androgyny and ego-consciousness, but let's explore it a bit and see what comes up.

Our earliest level of experience of this world is the experience of being unified with our mother in the ocean of the womb. Our nutrition and blood circulation in foetal existence depends utterly on our connection with our mother's body via the umbilical cord. We are separated at birth, the umbilical severed, but the new world we are delivered into, the 'external' world, is in a sense another womb. "Birth is to come out of a womb; and to go into a womb." (Brown) The idea that the material world is our mother is found in archaic Earth-Mother beliefs; in psychoanalysis, where exploration of the external world is seen as a symbolic exploration of the insides of the mother, where "Geography is geography of the mother's body" (Brown); and in language, where the word 'matter' derives from the Latin *mater*, mother.

Tantric cosmology sees the ground of existence as the union of the male and female principles, Shiva and Shakti. The manifest world is the product of their interplay, where Shiva is the static principle of consciousness and awareness, and the female Shakti is the dynamic principle of energy and manifestation. This is very similar to the Vedic idea of *maya*, or illusion. The 'material' world is seen as an illusion weaved by the goddess Maya (incidentally, also the name of the Buddha's mother), behind which lies the non-manifest reality of cosmic consciousness. We can also relate this back to the idea that Satan rules the world of manifestation—"The Devil is the lord of the world" (Luther)—and God rules the 'non-material' realm of the 'spirit'. Tantra's Shiva-Shakti cosmology is much more holistic, and does not treat the web of matter weaved by Shakti as 'illusory' in the sense of something to be overcome, some cosmic deception that inhibits us. It is seen as the basis of our spiritual quest, the 'raw material' with which we should work to transmute ourselves and the world.

We are, at present, part of the Earth. This planet doesn't 'stop' at the ground we stand on—its true boundary is the outer edge of the atmosphere, and we are thus *inside* the Earth. And, like the human body, the Earth's body doesn't really 'end' in an absolute way at its boundary, or skin. The atmosphere, like the skin, is a bridge as well as a barrier, mediating the transmission of many forms of energy and matter—most notably light and heat—between the planet and the solar system, and the rest of the universe.

The transition from seeing our human mother as our Mother to seeing the world, or the Earth, as our Mother, is central to initiatory rites. In many tribal societies, pubescent initiates are isolated from their biological families. Mothers often grieve, seeing the initiation as a literal death of their child—and the birth of an independent adult. Many initiations take place in subterranean environments—caves or holes in the ground—from which the initiate emerges as a child of the Earth. It is from such underground wombs that mythologies involving the labyrinth as an initiatory complex emerge. In cultures where male-only initiatory societies emerged, the process often became a way of appropriating the power of the mother, and reveals another example of ritual androgyny:

> *"The young man is put into a hole and reborn—this time under the auspices of his male mothers." Male mothers; or vaginal fathers: when the initiating elders tell the boys "we two are friends," they show them their subincised penis, artificial vagina, or "penis womb." The fathers are telling the sons, "leave your mother and love us, because we, too, have a vagina." Dionysus, the god of eternal youth, of initiation, and of secret societies was twice-born: Zeus destroyed his earthly mother by fire, and caught the baby in his thigh, saying: "Come enter this my male womb."*

Norman O. Brown, Love's Body

To a certain extent, though, all this is still abstraction. The transition from a 'biological' to a 'spiritual' mother is as useless and alienating as the Christian spiritual Father concept if our cosmic parent is envisaged in terms of an abstract deity. The importance of 'rebirth' is in the rebirth of awareness, the emergence of a feeling that we are fused with, and part of our environment. For the foetus, the fusion with the mother is an obvious fact that is not recognized with conscious clarity, because of an undeveloped sense of awareness and the fact that no other state has been experienced. Our fall from union seems to facilitate—via contrast and separation—a heightened awareness of reality, through which subsequent re-union with the environment may be experienced with greater intensity. "For I am divided for love's sake, for the chance of union." (Crowley, *The Book of the Law*)

Since we are dealing with the relationship between human consciousness and the environment, one of the most important areas of interest here is what is commonly known as earth mysteries. This is the investigation of human interaction with the natural landscape in terms of spirituality, especially regarding sacred sites, whether these sites occur naturally or are constructed. There is usually a dualism at work in the investigation of sacred sites, with the scientific disciplines of archaeology, anthropology and ethnography on one side, and paganism, psychology and spirituality on the other. The 'subjective' side (pagan investigators interested in the past and present use of such sites) is necessarily full of speculation and assumptions—my own writings included—but it does hold the key to approaching an understanding of stone circles, burial complexes, standing stones and all other such sites. That is, *the function of sacred sites cannot be understood without an understanding of (which must include an experience that approaches) the mind-set of the people who built them.* This task is probably impossible if taken to be a 'perfectible' scientific project, but we have much greater access to archaic states of consciousness than we are led to believe.

In trying to convey the idea that the LSD experience can access different modes of consciousness from along the evolutionary line, Timothy Leary quotes the German anthropologist Egon Freiherr von Eickstedt, offering it for comparison with documented accounts of LSD sessions. Von Eickstedt is trying to describe his idea of the spiritual attitude of australopithecines, our early ancestors:

> *In the way of experience there is dominant, throughout, a kaleidoscopic interrelated world. Feeling and perception are hardly separated in the world of visions; space and time are just floating environmental qualities … Thus the border between I and not-I is only at the border of one's own and actually experienced, perceptible world.*

In other words, for pre-hominid apes, and for the earliest humans, the definition of personal identity could be expressed as: I am my experience. This obviously includes the perceptible landscape, so any sacred sites and constructions that predate the evolution of ego-psychology in human cultures should be considered in these terms. This intertwining of human identity and nature is given a more roundabout, but somewhat fuller expression by Chris Knight in *Blood Relations*:

> *In this scheme of things [that of Australian Aborigines], human and natural cycles of renewal are mutually supportive and sustainable through the same rites. The skies and the landscape are felt to beat to human rhythms. Everything natural, in other words, is conceptualised in human terms, just as everything human is thought to be governed by natural rhythms.*
>
> *… There seems no reason to discount the Aborigines' own belief that in their rituals they were drawing upon natural rhythms and harmonising with them to the advantage of their relationship with the world around them. It was not that man was dominating nature; but neither was it that human society stood helpless in the face of nature's powers. Rather, human society was flexible enough and sensitive enough to attune itself finely to the rhythms of surrounding life, avoiding helplessness by replicating internally nature's own 'dance'. Nature was thereby humanized, while humanity yielded to this nature. If the hills felt like women's breasts, if rocks felt like testicles, if the sunlight seemed like sexual fire and the rains felt like menstrual floods, then this was not mere 'projection' of a belief system onto the external world. This was how things felt—because given synchrony and therefore a shared life-pulse, this was at a deep level how they were.*

Naturally, the experience of a psychedelic trip does not reproduce the *actual* mind-set of archaic humans. For us, a trip stands only in relation to our everyday, 'normal', experience of the world, and is quite different from the continuous, everyday experience of, say, a Neolithic Avebury resident, for whom such a world-view may be 'normal'. Nevertheless, such experiences, induced by chemicals or otherwise, should stand as the cornerstone of our understanding of sacred sites—and pre-civilised culture in general. And in any case, we shouldn't be interested in trying to replicate the mind-set of archaic humanity. Individual initiation isn't a simple one-way 'return to the womb', but a more highly evolved sense of omni-directional unity that follows the experience of division. Similarly, any attempt to re-engineer our culture's experience of the environment, inspired by prehistoric and existing 'primitive' cultures, should be a return to a similar point, but higher up on the evolutionary spiral. "We are not interested in a return to the primitive, but a return *of* the primitive, inasmuch as the primitive is the repressed." (Hakim Bey)

My conception of the Goddess, then, has less to do with a visualized representation of a vast cosmic woman, ox, or serpent than it has to do with my immediate, moment-to-moment experience of the world I am part of.[7] Even in my Kundalini dream, the 'presence' of the Goddess was an intuited fact, not a confrontation with a manifest form. The two instances of feeling Her presence were both experiences of intense body sensations and energy rushes, accompanied by the self-evident dream-conviction that this *was* the Goddess. In waking life, this perception arises very much along the lines of Phil Hine's idea that Kundalini is associated with "one's physical sensation of the here & now". This sensation is not a narrow feeling of mundanity, not the dissipation of mystery and numinosity that is usually associated with the apt phrase "down to earth". It

> "Mariners sailing close to the shores of Tuscany heard a voice cry out from the hills, the trees and the sky: "The Great God Pan is dead!" Pan, god of panic. The sudden awareness that everything is alive and significant. The date was December 25, 1 AD. ... The final apocalypse is when every man sees what he sees, feels what he feels, hears what he hears... The creatures of all your dreams and nightmares are right here, right now, solid as they ever were or ever will be..." (William S. Burroughs, *Apocalypse*)

7. This iconoclastic attitude might be taken as a refutation of the "personifying" element of the animism I currently espouse. In fact, it expresses it with sophistication. As James Hillman says in *Pan and the Nightmare*, "When Pan is alive then nature is too, and it is filled with Gods, so that the owl's hoot *is* Athene and the mollusc on the shore *is* Aphrodite. These bits of nature are not merely attributes or belongings. They are the Gods in their biological forms. ... Whatever was eaten, smelled, walked upon or watched, all were sensuous presences of archetypal significance." I'm now more out of phase with my monotheistic tendencies here than with the iconoclasm. [2007]

is exactly the opposite: a sense of the intense completeness and fullness of each moment; a paradoxical but perfectly natural feeling of being totally grounded, yet adrift in a vertiginous whirlpool of possibilities.

A related point that interests me is that investigations into the function and purpose of archaeological artifacts are nearly always governed by the sacred/profane dualism. Is this antler-pick just a common tool, or did it have ritual significance? Are these cave paintings just 'art' (in the modern, profane, sense of 'representation'), or were they part of a system of hunting 'magic'? It's clear that *somewhere* the rigid distinction between the 'sacred' and 'profane' arose. Otherwise, we wouldn't be in the present situation where for most people the 'sacred' only exists in church on Sundays (if sacredness exists at all). According to Alan Watts, 'profane' didn't always mean irreligious or blasphemous. It merely signified "an area or court before (*pro*) the entrance to a temple (*fanum*). It was thus the proper place of worship for the common people as distinct from the initiates, though here again the 'common' is not the crude but the communal—the people living in society. By contrast, the sacred was not the merely religious but what lay outside or beyond the community, what was—again in an ancient sense—extraordinary or outside the social order." (*Nature, Man & Woman*)

Judging from this, the sacred/profane duality arose as a result of the increase in human populations. Beyond a certain point, it seems that the full power and mystery of existence, as felt by the earliest humans, could not be a constant fact of everyone's experience if "social order" was to evolve. Even beyond this point, it can be seen from Watts' argument that the sacred/profane distinction didn't necessarily mean that everyday experience was utterly bereft of spiritual significance. This spiritual poverty, this rigid division of life into the sacred and profane (in their modern senses), has only been the norm of human experience for several hundred years, if that. And in their historical accounts, modern scientists have been projecting this division back in time for far too long. A re-vision of anthropology and archaeology is overdue, necessary and, I feel, imminent.

It seems ridiculous that anyone could assume that prehistoric humans sectioned life into neat compartments, mundane and extraordinary, profane and sacred, with anything like the rigour and inflexibility that the modern West does. Only affluent cultures, where day-to-day survival is not really a pressing issue, can even *afford* such a distinction. For pre-civilised (i.e. before cities) societies, where existence was dynamic and unstable, life depended on crops and crops depended on weather, among other things. For pre-agricultural societies, life depended on the gathering of food and the hunting of animals, which are subject to even more unstable factors. And these things, agriculture and hunting, were the prime focus for 'religious' activity. Gods and goddesses of the hunt, gods and goddesses of the Earth and crops dominated their relationship with the divine. What we consider the 'mundane' bits about life, like fuelling our bodies and keeping warm, were for these people projects loaded with importance and significance. In such a society, there's nothing more significant than staying alive. Thus food, shelter, hunting, farming, communication, the sharing of knowledge and skills, all were imbued with what we would consider 'spiritual' significance.

The figure of the shaman, "technician of the sacred", stands as the first step in the progressive division of life into the sacred and the profane, but the first shamans could only have stood "outside the social order" in a shallow sense. Early shamans would have depended on the social order for basic support and a purpose for their path's numerous trials, and the society would have depended on them for communication with deities and spirits, or forces of nature—more often than not for the governing and aiding 'mundane' projects like hunting and farming.

In short, life was a unity. Everything depended on everything else. The body was divine, and experience of the body included the environment. For ourselves, living in a culture where the dominant spiritual institutions have insisted not only on separating themselves from everyday life, but directing their spiritual aspirations *outside this world*, it's evident that a new vision of spirituality more directly concerned with life, the Earth, our bodies and *survival* is needed. We cannot live on bread alone, but I don't want to try to live without it. It's no coincidence that it took an affluent society like our own, where day-to-day existence is taken for granted, to produce a device capable of utterly destroying the biosphere.

Books Used/Sampled

Thus Spoke Zarathustra by Friedrich Nietzsche

The Gay Science by Friedrich Nietzsche

Ecce Homo by Friedrich Nietzsche

Nietzsche: Philosopher, Psychologist, Antichrist by Walter Kaufmann

Janus: A Summing Up by Arthur Koestler

William Blake: Selected Poems edited by P.H. Butter

The Tree of Lies by Christopher S. Hyatt

Pacts with the Devil by S. Jason Black & Christopher S. Hyatt**

The Devil's Notebook by Anton Szandor LaVey

The Secret Life of a Satanist by Blanche Barton

The NOX Anthology: Dark Doctrines edited by Stephen Sennitt*

Towards 2012 part II: Psychedelica edited by Gyrus

Life Against Death by Norman O. Brown*

Love's Body by Norman O. Brown**

Nature, Man & Woman by Alan Watts*

The Goddesses and Gods of Old Europe by Marija Gimbutas*

The Avebury Cycle by Michael Dames**

Blood Relations: Menstruation and the Origins of Culture by Chris Knight**

The White Goddess by Robert Graves

Tantra: The Indian Cult of Ecstasy by Philip Rawson*

The Tantric Way by Ajit Mookerjee & Madhu Khanna*

Kundalini, Evolution & Enlightenment edited by John White

Magick by Aleister Crowley

The Book of the Law by Aleister Crowley

Re/Search: Modern Primitives edited by V. Vale & A. Juno**

The Holy Bible edited by the Christian Church

Meditations on the Apocalypse by F. Aster Barnwell

The Supernatural by Colin Wilson

The Wise Wound: Menstruation & Everywoman by Penelope Shuttle & Peter Redgrove**

Men, Women & Chainsaws by Carol. J. Clover

Lame Deer: Seeker of Visions by John (Fire) Lame Deer and Richard Erdoes

Yoga: Immortality and Freedom by Mircea Éliade

Gods of Love and Ecstasy: The Traditions of Shiva and Dionysus by Alain Daniélou*

Dictionary of Gods and Goddesses, Devils and Demons by Manfred Lurker

Secrets of Mayan Science/Religion by Hunbatz Men

The History of Magic by Eliphas Lévi

The Psychedelic Reader edited by Timothy Leary, Ralph Metzner and Gunter M. Weil

Dead City Radio by William S. Burroughs (spoken word cassette)

T.A.Z. by Hakim Bey (spoken word CD)

* recommended in relation to the ideas discussed in this essay
** bloody essential

Related Films

The Wicker Man directed by Robin Hardy

The Divine Horsemen by Maya Deren

Videodrome by David Cronenberg

Crash by David Cronenberg

Santa Sangre by Alejandro Jodorowsky

Carrie by Brian de Palma

Alien³ by David Fincher

The Exorcist by William Friedkin

The Last Temptation of Christ by Martin Scorcese

Dracula by Francis Ford Coppola

The Hunger by Tony Scott

Picnic at Hanging Rock by Peter Weir

Journey to the Centre of the Earth by Henry Levin

Ginger Snaps by John Fawcett

THE GODDESS IN WHARFEDALE

*This was my first attempt at getting my research surrounding the prehistoric rock
art of Rombald's Moor, West Yorkshire, in print. It was published in* HEAD
*magazine issue 8 (1997), edited by Holly Mina. While compiling this turbulent
rush of investigation and inspiration, I realised that despite the wilfully
idiosyncratic nature of the style, there were some genuine new discoveries about
the history of the region emerging. These were compiled into the booklet* Verbeia,
*using the pseudonym G.T. Oakley (see http://dreamflesh.com/projects/verbeia/).
That booklet remains the most "accurate" source of information on the topics discussed here; this article retains more of the original gnostic fire of discovery. Many
thanks to the Manor House Museum (Ilkley), the Local History Library (Leeds),
the SEC Library (Avebury), Paul Bennett's Library (Bennett's bedroom), and
UBIK Books (Leeds, RIP). Dedicated to Harry Speight.*

*Firewoman, river of life / Firewoman, mother and eye / Firewoman, seeding below
/ Firewoman, help my earth glow*

Psychic TV, 'Firewoman'

A T FIRST it was just the stones.
  The north side of Rombald's Moor, steep crags and patches of forest,
towers over the town of Ilkley in West Yorkshire. Scattered over its hills are
literally hundreds of prehistoric rock carvings that are still baffling archaeologists and
students of the history of art. They are all seemingly abstract, dominated mainly by

'cup-and-ring' designs. Cup-like depressions carved into the rock, alone or clustered in groups, often surrounded by one or more rings. These rings may overlap with those radiating out from nearby cups; there may also be a straight groove running from the central cup, out across the rings.

After checking these out for a while, I was amazed to learn that nearly identical carvings exist in Northumberland, across Scotland and Ireland, Portugal, Italy and Scandinavia. Closely related 'primitive art' can also be found in the Canary Islands, Africa, India, Australia, the Americas, and many others places I'm sure. Across the globe, these enigmatic designs can date to anywhere from the Stone Ages to the present day (in the case of tribal cultures still making them). The ones in Ilkley are hard to date, because of their exposure to the elements, and guesses range from Neolithic times (5000-2000 BCE) to the late Iron Age (about 500 BCE).

I was initially attracted to these markings *because* of their enigma. The possible significance of megalithic sites like Stonehenge seemed to me to be all mapped out, exhaustively elaborated. Yet stabs at the meaning of cup-and-ring marked rocks are generally half-hearted, quelled by a lack of reference points. Ronald Morris lists *104* possible interpretations, all extremely brief, in his book on the rock art of Galloway— from the stupidly prosaic ("stone age doodles") to the wildly improbable ("carved by lasers from outer space").

Several people have grappled with interpreting the carvings in an open-minded and intelligent way, but they are few. For good reason. *We will never know what these carvings meant or were used for.* This is the bottom line of most prehistoric investigations. We'll never know, not exactly. How you proceed from this baseline of ignorance is a mark of your own psyche. Do you not even start to delve further, dismayed by the prospect of never being able to attain certainty? Do you meticulously catalogue that which you can be certain of, sites and sizes, recurrent features? Or do you, in wilful ignorance of the evidence that exists, treat prehistoric art as some sort of Rorschach for your own mind, projecting your desires onto them to suit your own needs?

Given that you're interested in rock art, the first option is an admission of despair, because ultimately nothing in life is certain. The second path is that of many academics, and such work is essential to any attempt at interpretation; but as an end in itself it is a petty cover-up for despair, and in omitting the realm of significance it removes genuinely human interests. The third tactic is a caricature of the independent 'mystical' researcher, and is how most academics would probably view my own work. But I think it has to be seen that an element of this subjective projection is unavoidable. As we have little concrete evidence about the meaning of prehistoric art, what else fills the gaps but

Achnabreck, Kilmartin, Scotland

Laxa das Rodas, Galicia, Spain

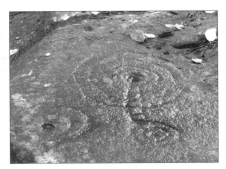

The Panorama Stone, Rombald's Moor, England

Roughting Linn, Northumberland, England

our own minds? In the interests of 'objectivity', the psychology of the prehistorian is left out of academic texts. Yet they are still people, and no amount of rigorous methodology can, I believe, erase the person from the writing. The fantasy of objective science is a contradictory enterprise of reality-denial: "I want to see the world as it would be if I were not here." The reality of the situation is that you're always there. In denying their own personal presence, many writers leave themselves (and their readers) open to an *unseen* subjectivity, which can either be uncovered and made part of the picture, or left to grow more powerful and malignant, eventually rigidifying into dogma.

My own personal approach is... personal. I have to experience the place I'm involved in. I spend time there and immerse myself in it, meditate and do rituals, note dreams and synchronicities. I bathe in the mystery until intuitions that make contact with intellect bubble up. I study a lot, and greatly value the work of historians and archaeologists. But I am not overly concerned with 'methodology'. My method is: go from the concrete part of reality that interests me, that draws me to it, and branch out into whatever different directions I feel are relevant. The 'disciplines' I delve into—archaeology, history, religion, etymology, ethnography—are subservient to the reality I'm investigating.

A general problem for me is deciding where I stand in relation to history. I feel I'm moving slowly (and non-linearly) towards a radical non-linear approach. I've tried to trace many different things through history, mainly shifting archetypal myth-figures; and I find too many cross-cultural connections, too many links across space and time to really believe, deep down, that 'history' (when it embraces human experience) can be accurately represented by a straight line. Historical context is important, but a wider context exists, that of the nature of time.

'Time' is a single word, but what it refers to is profoundly diverse and chaotic.

Linear historical time: One day, year, century after another, ad infinitum.

Linear eschatological time: One day, year, century after another... BANG!!!

Cyclical time: Each day is created anew at daybreak; each year is, in a way, the first. The growing-older-and-dying world co-exists with the Dreamtime, where all the ancestors are still active and all myths and realities recur.

Cyclical eschatological time: "Anyone who can read history with both hemispheres of the brain knows that a world comes to an end every instant ... And every instant also gives birth to a world—despite the cavillings of philosophers & scientists whose bodies have grown numb—a present in which all impossibilities are renewed, where regret & premonition fade to nothing in one presential hologrammatical

psychomantric gesture." (Hakim Bey)
Real time: No such thing!

All forms of time are potentially accessible. Many different gradations of these simplified categories are usually experienced in the course of a day by most people, but the subtle differences usually go unnoticed.

So history is not absolute. History as we know it is our own culture's *construct* of time, our largely linear map of temporality, projected back onto the material artifacts left in the fabric of the world by our ancestors. Not to mention the psychological prejudices and models we leave unquestioned, and our lack of culturally sanctioned landmarks in the realm usually called the 'spiritual'—a realm that was arguably a prime concern for 'map-makers' in prehistory. 'Objective history' is an illusion born of a lack of true context, our ontological context.

One of the stickiest problems in tracing mythology and religious practices through history is that of tracing influence and co-mapping meaning. Should we compare similar motifs and artifacts across time and space in our search for meaning? For example, could the recent rock art of the !Kung San bushmen in Africa have any bearing upon the carvings left on Rombald's Moor by people who lived thousands of years ago?

Things become stickier (for the linear historian) when times and places are closer together, but no direct evidence of cross-cultural interchange appears to exist. The Swastika Stone near Ilkley is pretty much identical to the 'Camunian Roses' in Val Camonica, Italy, and they were possibly carved within 500 years of each other. Did the two cultures that produced these designs interact? Was there a parallel, but separate evolution of the same basic pan-European design, the crossed circle? Was it coincidence? If so, is the meaning of each necessarily as separate as the carvings themselves? And do we need to insult the critical judgement of readers by meticulously pointing out the subtle differences between similar symbols, and only tentatively making comparisons? It is ironic that, because of their pedantic methodologies, texts aimed at the academic community (a most discerning and critical bunch), demand the least amount of critical intervention on the part of the reader.

I do not unquestioningly believe in Jung's theory of 'universal archetypes', but I do believe in the uniformity of basic human physiology, and I think the body is one of the main aspects of the world from which maps of the spirit—shamanism, alchemy, yoga, tantra, whatever—unfold. So we may expect some recurring global motifs in art and myth, notwithstanding the infinite variations that similar body-minds interacting with different environments produce.

I also believe that we each need to ask ourselves why we are interested in these things. What do I get out of this? I have no illusions (OK, a few) that I'm trying to contribute to some ever-progressing body of human knowledge. The feeling that we're building up an increasingly accurate and 'truthful' picture of the world as time goes by is part of the linear history package. Look at the ridiculous ideas held by quite intelligent people in the past, and assume that your own ideas may be equally stupid in the end.

In the end? What end? The straight line is hard to shake off...

There's one thing I'm definitely not in this for. I don't claim to be *right*. I get enough out of it already, and don't need gaps in my enjoyment to be filled with the consensus of agreement. I have to write this, and hope some people get stimulated by it. But... "I am not interested in the academic status of what I am doing because my problem is my own transformation." (Michel Foucault) I involve myself in the conscious recognition of what I project onto the past. My theories will have a different emphasis from others' because my transformation is different. Why shouldn't people print for themselves a license to steal from the past, as Hakim Bey phrases it, as long as they're conscious that they may have no 'real' connection to the culture they plunder, or to academic history? This is the Chaotic approach to history, the utilization of any and all human cultural artifacts for the purpose of making life *now* more interesting, stimulating and challenging. It can be abused by those who trivialize or entirely misappropriate other cultures, possibly affecting the general view of that culture; or by those who fail to keep a check on their ego and their connection with the here-and-now of their lives. It can also be used as the most adaptable and dogma-free map-making tool around. Flexible enough to cope with inevitable change, ontologically rigorous enough to realize it's never *right*, never authoritative, always capable of laughing at itself. As a friend once said, some people would rather be right than happy.

THE FIRST TIME I visited the Badger Stone on Rombald's Moor, I walked alone across the moors with a map. As I crossed a small valley, clouds gathered and light rain fell. I put the map away and stumbled across the heather shrouded in mist. As I blindly approached the stone, the rain fell harder, and all I could see around me was thick white moving mist. By the time I reached it, and rounded it to see the carvings, I was too wet to care about the rain, a state which alters consciousness into a more receptive mode. Throughout my explorations of the moors, I've found that there has been a subtle interactivity between the land, my consciousness and the weather, as if

The Badger Stone, Rombald's Moor

all conspire to make me receptive to a new discovery. Standing in front of the ancient carvings on this stone, I was struck by the realization that something I considered exotic and alien, something only found in caves in remotest Australia, was actually here as well, just down the road. The rock carvings are always more impressive when they're wet, and this, one of the most impressive set of carvings on the moor, made quite an impression on me. I did some spontaneous chanting and whirling, then walked away. As I left the stone, the mists began to clear, and the rain stopped abruptly.

Later in the year, I was writing about my idea that the Christian Satan is a demonized remnant of prehistoric chthonic snake-goddesses. Flicking through a book on folklore, I found a picture of an altar stone showing the goddess Verbeia. She holds two snakes, and now stands in the All Saints Parish Church in Ilkley. The mythic irony was too much, I had to check it out. I had only the faintest idea that she would lead me back up on to the moors, and deeper into the stones.

Verbeia

KNOWN ONLY THROUGH a dedication to her, carved by the Prefect of the Second Cohort of Roman troops stationed in Ilkley during 3rd century CE, and her depiction on a separate altar stone (right). The All Saints Church stands on the remains of the Roman fort. The dedication (which can now be seen in the Manor House Museum behind the church) reads: "To Verbeia. Sacred. Clodius Fronto. Ded. Prefect of the Cohort, Second Lingones."

Goddess of the River Wharfe, which flows down from the Pennines in the northwest, through Ilkley at the bottom of the valley which the moor overlooks, and east

The altar stone in All Saints Church, Ilkley

to the Humber estuary. Snakes and flowing water have intimate archaic connections. The two snakes held by Verbeia probably represent the two streams that flowed from the moor in Roman times, past either side of the fort enclosure, and into the Wharfe.

The Roman troops stationed here were only Roman in political allegiance. Racially, the Lingones were Celtic Gauls recruited from the upper Marne in eastern France. A goddess image similar to Verbeia—she holds two snakes and has a pleated skirt—was found in Mavilly, which is in the region where the Lingones cohort were recruited from. In this area, Gaulish Celts are known to have been greatly concerned with water cults. Mavilly is only 35 miles south of the famous healing spring at the source of the Seine. Did the troops bring a goddess-related water cult with them to blend into the matrix of the Wharfedale environment?

Scholars argue against a Celtic origin for the word 'Verbeia'. But a female water divinity holding snakes would, in nature if not in name, happily dovetail with the way in which the native Celts of northern England (the Brigantes) probably made their environment sacred. Water cults were very frequent among the Celts: they cast offerings into wells and lakes, including human heads (Celts, like the Greeks, believed the head to be the seat of life-force, as the 'head' of a river is its source). Romans likewise would sanctify natural features; for them, "every grove, spring, cluster of rocks or other significant natural feature had its attendant spirit. Generally the locals gave such entities personal names, but a stranger ignorant of these would refer to each

The Mavilly goddess

simply as *genius loci*, 'the spirit of the place'. Especially awe-inspiring or beautiful spots possessed proportionately powerful genii." (Ronald Hutton) Verbeia seems likely to be a fusion of existing Brigantian and imported Gaulish and Roman influences.

Sifting through languages to find the origins of 'Verbeia' proved to be a dizzying task. Even a firm knowledge of linguistic influences in the area at that time wouldn't stop your head from spinning. Two possibilities: Either language, like the universe, plays tricks, and leads you around in baffling cycles which appear connected to every other cycle; or the name 'Verbeia', for whatever reasons, happens to be an inexplicably polysemic (many-meaninged) cross-linguistic condensation of some of our most primal intuitions about nature. Follow me...

Spring

VERBEIA IS OFTEN equated with Brighid, the Irish goddess, a.k.a. Bridget, Bride, Bríd or Bríg—possibly the origin of Brigantia, the goddess of the Brigantes. Bride's Day is Imbolc, 1st February, or when the ewes start to lactate. A goddess who heralds the coming warmth of spring. The Mavilly goddess is shown surrounded by rising vegetation. The Latin for spring is *ver*, from which our 'vernal', 'verdigiris' (green rust on copper) and 'verdant' (fresh, green) come. A botanical term, 'vernation', refers to the arrangement of leaves in a bud. This derives from the Latin *vernatio*: the flourishing renewal of plants in spring, and the snake's sloughing of skin in spring. All these spring-associated Latin words stem from the Indogermanic root √WES, meaning "to shine".

Fire

BRIGHID PRESIDES OVER FIRE. Goddess of blacksmiths. Brighid, from *brigh*, 'strength'. Welsh *bri* means 'power', and *brig* means 'hill-top' ('Brighid' and 'Brigantia' are often translated as 'The High One'). Ancient belief in the sacred power of hills and mountains… the lighting of fires on hill-tops at seasonal festivals… St Bridget (the Christian edition) was honoured by nuns at a monastery in County Kildare, who kept her sacred flame burning until the Reformation. The public shrine to Vesta, Roman goddess of fire, both domestic and ritual, was a sacred fire tended by the Vestal Virgins. Brighid, too, ruled over the domestic hearth, and in Gaelic Scotland her bird was the white swan. 'Swan Vestas' anyone?

'Vesta' and close-to-home words like 'vernacular' both derive from the same Indogermanic root as all the shining spring-like words—√WES can also mean 'dwell, live, be'. Home and fire, dwelling and light. From the temporary base-camp hearths of the first proto-human hunter-gatherers through to the Celts and the Roman Empire, these two are intertwined.

The most famous stones on the moor are the Cow & Calf—the 'Cow' is a vast part of a rocky outcrop overlooking Ilkley, the 'Calf' is a smaller, though still large boulder that has apparently separated from the crags. The larger rock was once known as the 'Inglestone Cow'. When Queen Victoria was crowned in 1838, "a great fire blazed on these famous stones, and Ilkley I am told, was 'illuminated.'" (Harry Speight)

There is a history of beacon hills in Wharfedale. During the early 19th century, when a French invasion was feared, beacon fires were tended all along Wharfedale. The beacon signal was sent from Ingleborough, over in the northernmost reaches of Ribblesdale (close to the Wharfe's source), down via various hills, including Beamsley Beacon just north of Ilkley, on to the Otley Chevin. Perhaps the prominent 'Inglestone Cow' was part of this network? The Scottish dialect word, *ingle*, 'fire burning on a hearth', may come from the Gaelic *aingeal*, meaning 'fire' or 'light'. The Mavilly goddess holds a torch as well as snakes.

The Cow & Calf rocks, Rombald's Moor

Milk

BRIGHID IS ALSO a cow goddess; she was reared on the milk of a white, red-eared cow. In Ireland, churn-staffs were fashioned into the likeness of a woman called Brìdeog, 'Little Bride'. 'Verbeia' may derive from the Old Irish root *ferb*, 'cattle', making her 'She of the Cattle'. Like the Irish Boand, 'She who has White Cows', goddess of the river Boyne. Like Marsa of Latvian mythological songs, "Mother of Milk, the Mother of Cows" (Marija Gimbutas), who may appear in animal stalls as a black snake.

The night before I read Gimbutas' book, where she relates Verbeia to Marsa, and suggests the *ferb* derivation, I was staying with friends who have two daughters. I dreamt I had breasts and was breast-feeding their two-year old.

There is strong evidence of an old calendar custom in the British Isles, around Beltaine or springtime in general, where the old fires are extinguished and new ones are lit. Cattle are then driven between two fires to divinely protect them from disease. 'Imbolc' means 'purification'. Inglestone Cow… Fire-stone Cow.

Ronald Morris found three separate people in Scotland who remembered from their youth a ritual connected to cup-marks in rocks. They would be filled with milk each spring, lest the "wee folk" prevent the cattle from giving milk that summer.

Water

"SPRINGS, WELLS AND RIVERS are of first and enduring importance as a focal point of Celtic cult practice and ritual." (Anne Ross) Not far from the Badger Stone, at the top of Heber's Gill, is a spring called Silver Well, "which it is not unlikely was an old Celtic tutelary spring, and bits of metal or other articles may have been thrown into it as offerings for protection from the saint or presiding genius of the well." (Speight)

The source of all life. We come from the ocean, we need water to live, we are two-thirds water. Verbeia, goddess of the river, bearing the two serpentine streams flowing down from the moor. They flow from the area where one finds the White Wells, a Victorian spa building. The healing powers of the spring waters on the moor here were reputed in the last century, and probably long, long before as well. Certainly the Romans were obsessed with spa baths, and there was one in Ilkley. "Verbeia may be a Latinised form of the Goidelic *guerif*, to heal." (Speight) *Geurir* is used in France with the same meaning.

(At the bottom of the bath in the White Wells today there is the familiar site of hundreds of coppers and ten pence pieces. You even find this in fountains in shopping malls. It is a remnant of the widespread Celtic practice, mentioned by Speight above, of casting offerings to water spirits into wells, lakes and rivers.)

> In Niederbronn, Alsace, where in Celtic times Diana was worshipped as the Goddess of sacred wells, to this day women carry water from the mineral spring to nearby mountains. There, they pour it over stones with circular depressions to ensure pregnancy. … Holy wells are recorded by the hundreds in 19th century literature. In Ireland, they mostly became St. Brigit's wells, all visited on the first day of spring. Devotees perform the rounds at such wells, washing their hands and feet and tearing off a small rag from their clothes, which they tie on a bush or tree overhanging the well. According to a 1918 written account from Dungiven parish, after performing the usual rounds at the well, devotees proceed to a large river stone which has footprints; they perform an oblation and walk around the stone, bowing to it and repeating prayers as at the well. If there are hollows or cupmarks in stones, the country people stoop to drink.
>
> Marija Gimbutas

Ronald Morris' survey of cup-and-ring marked stones in Argyll, Scotland, revealed that they "are nearly always carved where there is a fine open view. … more often than not it includes a view of sea or estuary." They are "nearly always made on parts of rock which are nearly *horizontal*. Thus, in southern Scotland seven out of eight sites have carved areas which are within 20 degrees of horizontal, and nearly half the carved areas are absolutely horizontal. ... Where there is a 'tail' or radial groove from near the middle of the cup-and-ring (very often from the cup), in about seven out of eight cases, where there is any slope on the rock surface, *the tail runs downhill*." This all accords well with the Ilkley carvings, which are dominant on the north side of the moor overlooking the river, and are often clustered close to springs or streams.

Before I had theorized about these glyphs, my intuitive 'offerings' to the Badger Stone consisted of pouring some of my drink (water or whiskey) into the cups and watching it stream down the grooves. There are *some* cups on near-vertical surfaces, but most were clearly meant to hold water, rain, or other fluids. Like wells, the water in cup-marks could be healing water. In regions where there are cup-marked rocks and peasant lore about them still survives, there are recurrent beliefs that water out of the cups is good for all manner of ailments, especially eye diseases.

The Greek Muses were water-nymphs, and poets drank from their springs on Mounts Helicon, Parnassus and Castalia for inspiration. To them, a poem was the water, honey or nectar of the Muses. Pythagoras gained prophetic insights from drinking spring water. Richard Onians, in his investigation of ancient Greek concepts about the body and soul, found that they believed 'life-essence' to be contained in a 'seed liquid' concentrated mostly in the cerebro-spinal marrow—"on tap in the genital and stored in the head", as Norman O. Brown puts it. They thought it came out of the body in the form of tears, sweat, and sexual fluids. Crying and sexual love are "repeatedly described as a process of 'liquefying, melting' ... Aristotle tells us that the region around the eyes was the region of the head most fruitful of seed, pointing to ... practices which imply that seed comes from liquid in the region of the eyes."

Tears, sex, melting... I think of Wilhelm Reich's ideas about bodily armour, rigid musculature softened by crying and sex. Experiences of weeping at orgasm. Tears, eyes, seed... the repressive myth of masturbation and blindness. There is an Egyptian myth of people coming out of a creator-god's eyes. Cup-marks, rain, creation, life-force, healing...

The Slavic goddess Mokosh-Paraskeva Pyatnitsa "is the dispenser of the water of life. ... The name *Mokosh* is connected with moisture, *mok-* or *mokr-* meaning 'wet, moist,' and her ritual was called *mokrida*. On the other hand, the root *mok-* appears as a name for stones. In Lithuanian, *mokas* is a 'standing stone,' always appearing in legends associated with lakes or rivers." (Gimbutas)

The significance of water and stones extends down into the rites of divine kingship.

Pagan British kings usually had to symbolically wed the goddess of the land. Even as late as the 17th century, England's King James said, "I am the husband, and all the whole island is my lawful wife." Gerald of Wales (12th century) said that in County Donegal, for his *feis* (inauguration), the king would bathe in water then stand barefoot in a footprint carved in rock, or sit on a stone to be handed his rod of office. The *feis* site of the Irish king O'Donnell in western Ulster was used until the end of the 16th century. It is a rock with the holy well Tobar an Duin at its foot, where the king probably bathed. In early Scottish history the fort of Dunadd, in the Kilmartin valley of Argyll, was one seat of the kingdom of Dalriada, "and upon the summit of the fortress the modern traveller can still find the carved footprint. Next to it in the rock surface is a bowl-shaped hollow and a splendid figure of a wild boar ... A ruler placing his foot in the print would be gazing north straight at the ancient row of megalithic monuments." (Hutton) "In Scandinavia engravings of human footprints are common—especially near the cupped stones. On the Bunsoh stones, indeed, footprints and cups are found together." (Herbert Kühn)

The king gains his power from his union with the goddess of the land, symbolized by his immersion in her waters and his body's shallow, but significant, penetration of her stones. Paul Devereux, in a persuasive book that links divine kingship back to shamanism, quotes a !Kung man talking of his trance experiences: "When people sing ... I dance. I enter the earth. I go in at a place like a place where people drink water. I travel a long way, very far. ... You enter, enter the earth, and you return to enter the skin of your body...". For the San people, snakes are significant because they enter the earth, go underground, like themselves when they go on ecstatic journeys.

J.D. Lewis-Williams suggests that rocks are 'veils' between this world and the spirit world, and that rock art is the destruction of this veil. "In many cultures, the shaman in his trance passes through the rock into the spirit world, and to communicate what had happened in the trance, the shaman depicts what had happened on the other side on the rock. ... The Hupa of America have a concept of spirits responsible for precipitation that live in the rock, and are known as 'Mi.' In addition, several contemporary shamans have acknowledged that the rock art is a marker for where a shaman could enter the rock." (Grant S. McCall)

Procreation

THE BELIEF SYSTEMS of the Australian aborigines, whose rock and totem-shield art is often compared to cup-and-ring markings, may be one of the most useful tools we have to approach the meaning of European petroglyphs. The Australian continent is their Bible; the earth, the physical landscape, embodies their spiritual understanding of the world, contains their history and knowledge. "Preliterate peoples are at pains to identify with their land as if it were a physiological or psychological 'echo' of themselves." (James G. Cowan) Body and earth, psyche and landscape.

Some hunter-gatherer tribes, like archaic humans, do not see sex and birth as cause and effect.[1] To explain birth, beliefs about the origin of children from the earth evolved. The spirits of unborn children dwell in the land, in rocks and pools, waiting to enter a receptive womb. Even after the connection between sex and birth is made, many, like the aborigines, favour the idea of earth-conception as ultimately essential to the creation of a child. Rocks or pools *"bore the spirit that would vitalise the baby.* It therefore seems likely that the purpose of cutting a circular cup in the surface of a rocky outcrop was to liberate a spirit and so ensure a complete and successful child-birth. ... At some later date a ring would be circumscribed about the cup to guarantee a second child, and in this way, as the years passed, the ring systems built up." (George Terence Meaden) This idea holds that the interlinking groups of cups and rings depict inter-family bonds. The 'spirits' released by carving the cup may have been those of ancestors as well as unborn children, for ancestors are frequently the source of divinatory and magical knowledge in shamanic cultures. For aborigines, the two types of spirit are interchangeable, as each person is a reincarnation of an ancestor.

Two apparent survivals of these notions in modern times. The Christian doctrine of baptism: a baby's soul is not 'saved' (and may as well not have one as far as hardcore Christians are concerned) until it is baptized, with holy water from a cup-shaped font. And the folklore of the stork, which carries babies from marshes to drop them down the chimneys of expectant parents.

The 'caged spirit' theory of cup-marked rocks does not 'explain' all the carvings, but no one 'explanation' will. The carvings were probably used by different people through time for different purposes; by different people across space for different purposes; and almost certainly by the *same* people for different purposes.

Our culture and our psyches, outside the frames and boundaries of 'art', are conditioned to assign singular meanings to symbols. Before dictionaries, words were a lot more elastic. Proto-linguistic symbol systems such as hieroglyphs were even more amenable to polysemy, the existence of many meanings. Further back in the development of symbols, petroglyphs take us into a realm of signification almost alien to

---

1. I wonder about this idea now—perhaps too much of a throwback to the "dumb primitives" view? Such people certainly wouldn't need a textbook to teach them about basic bodily processes. [2007]

the industrialized west. Their meanings seem abstract and vague until they are bound to the concrete feelings and bodily, non-verbal perceptions they refer to. And many meanings happily co-exist, emanating from the same symbol without being stifled by fear of paradox.

Vertex

MIDDLE ENGLISH *hwerfen*, 'turn, change'. Spelt in The Ormulum by Ormin (12th century Lincolnshire) as *wharfen*. The variations are endless: *hweorfa*, 'whirl, what is hastily turned around'; *hweorfan*, 'a turning, winding round', cognate with Norse *hvarf*, 'a sharp bend'; Old Norse *hwerfi*, 'bend, crook'. Among these words is certainly the origin of, or a major influence on 'Wharfe', which turns and winds along the valley floor before and after Ilkley.

'Verbeia' has always been related to 'Wharfe', and a trip back to the *ver-* words in Latin gives us, if not a confirmation of the link, at least some fruitful and irresistibly fascinating associations. Many of our own *ver-* words come from the Latin *vertere*, 'to turn'. 'Vertebra' means 'something to turn on', describing the backbone's interlocking pivotal structure. 'Vertex' is 'the highest point'; in anatomy it refers to the crown of the head, where hair spirals. Latin *vertex* literally means 'that which turns', but can refer to 'top, crown, summit, pole, whirl; whirlpool, eddy'. Properly it refers to the turning point, especially the Pole Star, around which all the others turn. 'Vertical' stems from these associations—straight up to, or down from, the crown or summit. 'Vortex' is a variant of 'vertex'. Dictionary definition: 'a mass of whirling fluid, whirlpool or whirlwind; a system viewed as swallowing up or engrossing those who approach it'. 'Whirl' is related to the Old Norse *hvirfill*, 'circle'; and, along with 'twirl', relates to the Gaelic *Tuirl*, 'to descend suddenly, to come down rapidly with a gyratory motion'. 'Vertigo' is from Latin *vertigo*, 'whirling', again from *vertere*.

The closest word I've found to 'Verbeia' in any language is from Anglo-Saxon, which couldn't have influenced the Roman altars in Ilkley—they invaded Britain after the Romans left. Nevertheless, the word *wer-bære* is 'a weir where fish are caught', which keeps the river connotations, as well as the idea of turning, as weirs (and wharves) redirect the flow of rivers.

'Verse' is another *vertere* word, because at the end of a line of poetry, one 'turns around' and starts a new one, unlike the linear flow of prose. Countless *–verse* words in English express contrary direction: converse, perverse, inverse, reverse, you get the idea.

Vertere itself comes from the Indogermanic root √WERT, 'to turn, become'. Also root of the Old English *wyrd*, 'destiny, fate, that which happens'. Sanskrit *vrt* means 'to turn, turn oneself, exist, be'.

Shamanism

BRIGHID, PATRONESS OF POETS & WRITERS, healers & doctors, and of black-smiths. Goddess of fire. She appears to be a late pagan distillation of the core elements of archaic shamanism.

The shaman is the original poet, the tribal myth-maker who pulls up a 'secret language' from the depths of ecstasy, the hidden roots of language.

The shaman is the healer *par excellence*, the witch-doctor.

A Yakut proverb says that smiths and shamans are from the same nest. Shamans often meet a smith during initiatory trances, who dismembers and then re-forges the shaman's body in his furnace. Both smiths and shamans are respected and often feared in Siberian tribes, because both possess esoteric transformative knowledge.

Most importantly, both are masters of fire. "Mastery over fire ... is a magico-mystical virtue that ... translates into sensible terms the fact that the shaman has passed beyond the human condition and already shares in the condition of 'spirits.'" (Mircea Éliade) Firewalking, eating hot coals, generating 'inner heat' for magical use, melting snow with will, drying wet sheets wrapped around the body while sat outside in freezing weather... Many tribes express magical power in terms of heat; Hindus call powerful divinities *jvalit*, 'possessing fire'; Indian Muslims in communication with God become 'burning'. The !Kung dance for hours around a fire to awaken *n/um*, a primal life energy that rests at the base of the spine and in the pit of the stomach. When it 'boils', it ascends the backbone, and when it reaches the skull, the shamanic *!kia* trance occurs. Those experiencing *!kia* can feel compelled to leap into the fire or handle the glowing embers.

Verbeia's equation with Brighid is poetically supported by her forest of linguistic associations: verse is the 'turning' form of poetry; we have the Goidelic *guerif*, to heal; both these aspects are deepened by her undoubted link with spring waters, inspiring and healing. Her fiery nature should be obvious by now.

Further, Verbeia's possible links to all the spiralling *vertere* words echoes one of shamanism's most basic features. The Centre of the World, the World Tree, Mountain or Pole, the shaman's path to the lower and upper realms of the other world. Through kundalini yoga, and the Greeks' cerebro-spinal 'life-force', this may be equated with the human spine. Raise the kundalini serpent to the crown chakra, through the vertebrae, past the crown of the skull, where hair spirals round in a vertex.

One impulsive evening I went up to the moor and spent the night alone at the Badger Stone. While drifting off, I opened my eyes suddenly and was startled beyond belief. One star in the sky was motionless, and all the others were drifting rapidly north across the sky. This persisted, as I stammered and reeled, for about 10 seconds. Then, in a gratefully received shift of perspective back to reality, I realized that the single 'star' was a satellite arcing across the sky. My mind, for some reason, had played the 'relative motion' trick you often get on trains, where the station appears to be moving when the train sets off.

Later that week, I was playing with a toy planetarium at a friends'—a small light over which you place a clear perspex hemisphere with all the constellations marked on it. I put it in a dark cupboard, and played with it by spinning the dome around. Instantly the memory of a dream (probably inspired by the shifting stars experience) from a night or two back flooded into me, and I had to stop turning the dome because of the dizzying memory rush. In the dream I was out in the open, and the entire night sky was revolving around one star above me, which was surrounded by bizarre light formations. Inspired by this, I searched out beliefs about the stars, particularly the Pole Star.

This is one of a few cards from the 'Vertical Oracle' divinatory deck (by Antero & Sylvi Alli) that arrived in the post shortly after I finished this writing. Make your own connections! For more information, see http://www.verticalpool.com.

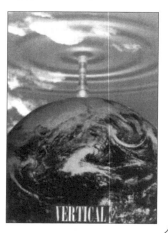

The Turko-Tatars, like a number of other peoples, imagine the sky as a tent ... In the middle of the sky shines the Pole Star, holding the celestial tent like a stake. The Samoyed call it the 'Sky Nail'; the Chuckchee and the Koryak the 'Nail Star.' The same image and terminology are found among the Lapps, the Finns, and the Estonians. The Turko-Altaians conceive the Pole Star as a pillar; it is the 'Golden Pillar' of the Mongols, the Kalmyk, the Buryat, the 'Iron Pillar' of the Kirgiz, the Bashkir, the Siberian Tatars, the 'Solar Pillar' of the Teleut, and so on. A complementary image is that of the stars as invisibly linked to the Pole Star. The Buryat

*picture the stars as a herd of horses, and the Pole Star ... is the stake to which they
are tethered.*

Mircea Éliade

Macrocosm is reflected in microcosm for such peoples, who identify the Sky Pillar
with the pole in the centre of their yurt or tent.

Ancient Saxons called the Pole Star *Irminsul*, termed 'the universal column which
sustains all', and passed the idea of the 'Pillar of the Sky' or 'Pillar of the World' on to the
Lapps of Scandinavia. Similar concepts survive in Romanian folklore. For Chuckchee
and Altaian shamans, the Pole Star is a hole in the sky through which they pass into
the upper levels of the spirit world.

My attention shifted from these findings to the Swastika Stone, a notable carving
found along the north side of Rombald's Moor. Nine cup-marks in a cross formation, surrounded by a whirl-
ing swastika groove, with a
curious appendage to one arm.
The north-south line of cups
is aligned to less than a degree
off magnetic north—pointing
straight at the Pole Star. This
connection was thrown a bit
by the fact that the swastika
appears to rotate in a clockwise
direction, whereas the stars in
the northern hemisphere go
anti-clockwise round the pole,
rising in the east and setting

The Swastika Stone, Rombald's Moor

in the west. But if it was meant to be some sort of connection between the earth and
the sky... Try pointing your finger north and making an anti-clockwise circle in the air,
following the stars. Imagine you are drawing a rotating disc. Now move your hand, the
disc, downwards until you are looking at the 'other side' of the disc, looking down your
finger instead of up it, but keeping it moving in the same direction. It will now appear
to be moving clockwise. If the stone describes the base of a Sky Pillar, extending down
from the Pole Star to the ground, the clockwise motion of the swastika makes perfect
sense—it maps the motion of the stars down onto the rock. Cup-and-ring petroglyphs
may be seen to echo the same image. The groove or 'tail' becomes the Sky Pillar, the cup

the Pole Star, and the rings the paths of the revolving stars.

(I should note here that I'm not moving towards the general idea that cup-and-ring patterns are maps of stellar constellations. Perhaps some involved rudimentary attempts at this, but no one seems to have found accurate correspondences in any existing patterns. They seem to be more to do with the sky as an access point to alternate realities.)

The swastika is a near-universal symbol that should be reclaimed from the Teutonic boot-boys of the mid-20th century. It is found in Buddhism and Hinduism, on goddess-related artifacts from Bronze Age Greece, and in British Celtic metalwork from the 1st century BCE. As a petroglyph, it is found in abundance in Val Camonica, northern Italy. Here there are 16 carvings almost identical to that near Ilkley, and 68 others with differing arm orientations, all spread over 27 rocks. They date from the 7th to the 1st century BCE. The symbol is also found in Sweden, along with many other designs based on the so-called Celtic Cross, the wheel with four spokes. "Across the Romano-Celtic world, from Britain to Czechoslovakia, the wheel was the symbol for the sky, representing either the sun alone, or the whole turning heaven." (Hutton) Most interpreters, indeed most surviving religions who still use it, see the swastika as a sun or fire symbol. Its connection with fire-oriented cults is strong, but the Ilkley carving is oddly positioned if it has anything to do with sun worship—it faces squarely north into the Wharfe valley. One possible sun connection exists, though. The 'appendage' cup, in relation to the central cup, is roughly aligned to the summer solstice sunrise in

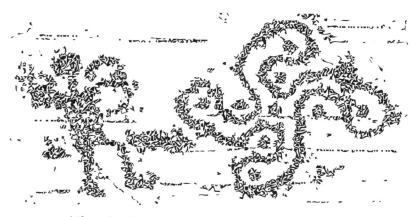

A 'Camunian Rose' Iron Age carving in Val Camonica, Italy, almost
identical to the Swastika Stone on Rombald's Moor, England

the northeast. The groove around it forms a sort of hook shape which, if turned in the same direction as the 'spin' of the swastika, would haul the solstice sun across the sky.

On the Isle of Man a Norse cross from around the 10th century was found standing in a groove in a large round stone in a churchyard. At its bottom is a fylfot, or swastika-like design, incorporating four spirals bound together. Of course, the national symbol of Man, the Three Legs, is a three-legged swastika.

A Norse fylfot from a cross in
Onchan, Isle of Man

February 1st in Man, until recently, was *Laa'l Breeshy*, 'Bridget's Feast Day' ('Wive's Feast Day' in northern England). A parish church, a nunnery, and no less than seven of the ancient keeils or cells on the Isle are named after the Irish saint. A favourite form of Bridget's Cross, central to Imbolc folk-rituals in Ireland, suggests a swastika.

Oddly, the Bible gives us a link between stones and ascension into the sky. Check out Genesis 28:10. Jacob spends the night in a place where he gathers stones together for pillows. "And he dreamed, and behold a ladder set up on the earth, and the top of it reached to heaven: and behold the angels of God ascending and descending on it." Vastly

Bridget's Cross

impressed by this place, he sets his pillow-stone up as a pillar, and anoints it with oil. He names the place *Beth-el*, 'sacred stone'.

"Throughout the world, certain images of ascent were used—the shaman's spirit could rise on smoke, ride along a rainbow, travel up a sunbeam and so on. But from northwest Europe to Tibet none was more ubiquitous than the ladder. … It shows the remarkably universal aspects of shamanism, then, that the image of a human figure atop a ladder occurs also in southern African rock art." (Devereux) The Zulu word form *-qab* associates trance-states with ascension and art: *ukutiqabu*, 'recovering from fainting'; *ukuqabela*, 'to climb to the top of a ladder, tree or mountain'; *ukuqabela*, 'to paint'.

In some cup-and-ring designs on Rombald's Moor, the single groove 'tail' becomes a ladder-like image.[2] The interlocking cup-and-rings may be series of levels of the spirit world penetrated by a shaman's consciousness. These varied and sometimes messy patterns evoke shamanism still evolving, humans repeatedly grappling with deep trance states, plumbing the depths behind and ascending the heights above the rocks, attempting to haul descriptions of their journeys back to the earth.

If this shamanic idea holds water, the dating of the moor's petroglyphs poses problems for the orthodox study of their significance. Most of the comparable Italian and Scandinavian glyphs are dated to the late Bronze Age or the Iron Age, the latter half of the 1st millennium BCE. Was there a Celtic or proto-Celtic shamanism that continued the traditions of much older cultures? Cup-and-rings appear in Neolithic tombs in Ireland. Paul Bennett, a local researcher who knows the moors here better than anyone I've met, believes the Swastika Stone could date to 2000 BCE or earlier—and its complexity suggests that the simpler cup-and-rings are even earlier.[3] People lived on Rombald's Moor from as early as 7000 BCE, so this is entirely possible.

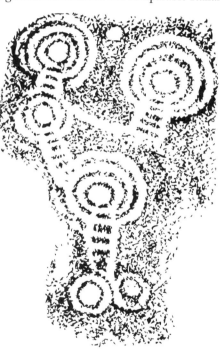

Most perplexing of all is the complex of shamanic associations constellated around Verbeia's possible etymologies. Possibly language playing tricks, but they're compelling tricks, evoking the vertical pillar up to the Pole Star... the ascent into a sky

Ladder-like carvings on the Panorama Stone, Rombald's Moor, opposite St Mary's Church

vortex, 'a system viewed as swallowing up or engrossing those who approach it'... vertebrae in the spine, the vertiginous whirling motion of a fiery climb to the vertex...

2. See Appendix II for a full discussion of the Rombald's Moor ladder carvings enigma. [2007]
3. The assumption that simpler designs designate an earlier origin for art is another inheritance of our culture's sense of linear historical progress that is sometimes misleading. [2007]

Liminality

I APPROACHED THE BADGER STONE once to do a brief ritual. As I neared it, it started to rain. I was reminded of my first visit, but I tried to shift my attention back to the present to focus on my ritual. After I started, I was soon forced back to the present. The rain pelted harder and harder, the wind grew more fierce, and at the peak of the ritual the rain turned into savage hail. It was blowing hard from behind me, hurting my head, and coming in at an almost horizontal angle, creating a tunnel-like effect before me—and an extremely conducive state of mind! I wound down, and the hail returned to rain. I left the site, and the rain stopped.

When the sun rose after I had the 'shifting sky' experience, just before it cleared the clouds on the horizon, it started to rain lightly. I jumped up to run for cover, but decided to stay and see the sun up with some chanting. It was beautiful. Glowing sun bursting up, gentle rain, and behind me a magnificent rainbow. I finished chanting, left, and the rain stopped. I kid you not.[4]

Memories of these experiences shouted for attention when I read Ruth White-house's book on cave-based cults in Neolithic central Italy, *Underground Religion*. The apparent sacred significance of water in 'abnormal states' (stalactites and stalagmites, bubbling or hot water, steam) to these people led her to recognize the importance of 'liminal' (marginal, borderline, cross-over) states in their beliefs. Cave mouths, between dark and light… stalagmites, hard water… steam, gaseous water… and ultimately the shaman, between this world and the other, a mediator. For numerous shamanic cultures, the rainbow is a prime liminal phenomenon, produced in the conjunction of sun and rain, fire and water, bridging the gap. Fire and water. Brighid. Verbeia. Why should they preside over such contradictory elements?

Atl-tlachinolli, Aztec hieroglyph for burning water

The Aztecs, according to Laurette Séjourné's *Burning Water*, believed that liberated conscious-ness could only be achieved through an internal bodily battle, a "blossoming war". Victory is at-tained through the union of opposites; the Aztec "vision of Earth as Paradise is based on the concept of the dynamic harmony between water and fire." Their hieroglyph for the "blossoming war" is called

4. An often uncanny synchrony between outdoor rituals and the weather has been a very frequent occurrence in all such work I've done since these early experiences. [2007]

atl-tlachinolli, from atl, 'water', and *tlachinolli*, 'something that has been burned'.

This symbol always accompanies Quetzalcoatl, the plumed serpent, the Aztecs' mythic originator. Bird-and-snake figures are frequent in myths across the globe, and probably represent the union of chthonic earthly realms (snake) with the skies above (bird). The Aztec symbol for the union of heaven and earth is the cross, perhaps the most basic possible representation of liminality (cross-over). The quincunx (a cross formed by five points, the four cardinal points and a centre) is "the most frequently occurring sign in the Meso-american symbolic language." The number 5 represents the centre, the point where heaven and earth meet, and the quincunx also symbolizes the heart, "the meeting-place of opposed principles". Curiously, one of their symbols for the Fifth Sun (or Era), the Sun of Movement, the Era of Quetzalcoatl, the unifying "Law of the Centre", is a swastika-like glyph.

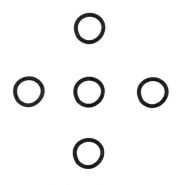

An Aztec quincunx

Aztec 'movement' hieroglpyh from Teotihuatecan

How all this spiritual cartography relates to human experience is crystallized for me in the Aztec vision of the heart as the centre, where opposites unite. We are impoverished if we can only feel one emotion at a time. All pure emotion, I find, is profoundly ambiguous. Polysemic. Anger and exhilaration, joy and bittersweet sadness, sexual bliss and terror, tender love and fear, weeping at orgasm… 'Emotions' are the words and concepts we tack on to the chaotic flows of psycho-biological energy around the body, flows which have no anchors and no true boundaries.

Potent emotion, when cut loose from judgement, becomes ecstasy.

References

T.A.Z. by Hakim Bey

Foucault edited by Lawrence D. Kritzman

The Pagan Religions of the Ancient British Isles by Ronald Hutton

Upper Wharfedale by Harry Speight

The Language of the Goddess by Marija Gimbutas

Pagan Celtic Britain by Anne Ross

The Origins of European Thought by Richard Broxton Onians

Love's Body by Norman O. Brown

The Prehistoric Rock Art of Argyll by Ronald W.B. Morris

The Rock Pictures of Europe by Herbert Kühn

One Medium, One Mind by Grant S. McCall
        (http://www.geocities.com/athens/forum/3339/rockart.html)

Shamanism and the Mystery Lines by Paul Devereux

The Aborigine Tradition by James G. Cowan

The Goddess of the Stones by George Terence Meaden

Shamanism by Mircea Eliade

Burning Water by Laurette Séjourné

An Algonkian Native American rock carving
in Peterborough, Ontario, Canada

ASPECTS OF
SHAMANISM

This was written during a period in 1998 when I came into contact with the academic end of what I was then obsessed with, the study of rock art and shamanism. A group of MA students from Southampton came up to Ilkley to investigate the area, and, with admirable openness, got in touch with the slightly-less-than-respected authorities on the region, myself and the wonderful Mr Paul Bennett. They were headed by Thomas Dowson, who co-wrote with David Lewis-Williams in 1988 a significant article titled 'The Signs of All Times: Entoptic Phenomena in Upper Palaeolithic Art'. When archaeological curmudgeon Paul Bahn made a thinly-veiled but scathing attack on Dowson's MA course (and students), I leaped to their defence with this piece that tried to remain as calm and academia-friendly as possible while still laying into the things I hate about it.

S HAMANISM IS THE SUBJECT of intense debate in many arenas at the moment, and here I wish to add my own idiosyncratic views.

First off, we have to remind ourselves of the origins of the word 'shaman'. It derives from *saman*, used by the Tungus people of Siberia, which means 'one who is excited, moved, raised.' Some think it derives in turn from an archaic Indian word meaning 'to heat oneself' or 'practice austerities'; others think it comes from a Tungus verb meaning 'to know' (Walsh 1990: 8). It was adopted—and made into an 'ism'—by anthropologists and ethnologists to refer to healers in various cultures who seemed to practice their art in similar ways. Mircea Éliade famously defined shamanism as 'techniques of ecstasy', highlighting its practical emphasis on entering altered states as a basic *modus operandi*. For a rule-of-thumb definition of shamanism, I prefer Walsh's slightly broader attempt:

> *Shamanism can be defined as a family of traditions whose practitioners focus on voluntarily entering altered states of consciousness in which they experience themselves or their spirit(s), traveling to other realms at will, and interacting with other entities in order to serve the community.*
>
> *ibid.*: 11

This is a good baseline, but as anyone who has studied the matter knows, there are many other elements to some of the traditions in this "family" that, while their occurrence may not be 100% ubiquitous and uniform, are widespread enough to warrant interest. I would say that the main such elements are the three-levelled cosmology, centred on an *axis mundi*; a focus on nature spirits (plant or animal) as guides or helpers; ritual incorporation of zoomorphic aspects into the shaman's identity ('shapeshifting', whether via costume or transformation of 'soul-image' during soul flight); initiation(s) via a breakdown / restructuring process; and so on.

There are too many cross-cultural parallels to document and categorize here, and this is precisely the heart of the debate around shamanism in many disciplines today: Similarity (comparison) vs. Difference (definition).

The Difference viewpoint often stems from a healthy awareness and celebration of human cultural diversity; respect for the idiosyncrasies of individual cultures is seen to be eroded by washing them away in a tide of Similarity. To me, the Difference/ Similarity debate (which I've polarized hideously here for the purposes of argument) is comparable to the old "The glass is half empty" / "The glass is half full" illustration of the difference between pessimism and optimism. The reality of the glass' situation is that both views are 'true', and they complement each other. So do Difference and Similarity, when seen as two perspectives on the same situation.

The !Kung and Kundalini

FOR INSTANCE, I am very struck by the similarities between descriptions given by the African !Kung San people of their entry into trance states, and the experience sought by Indian tantrikas practising Kundalini yoga. Tantrikas say that the Kundalini Sakti, a feminine 'serpentine' life-force lying coiled and dormant at the base of the spine, rises up the spine when aroused, eventually uniting with Siva at the crown chakra (Mook-erjee & Khanna 1977: 21). The experience is usually one of an "explosion of psychic heat" (*ibid.*: 193). The !Kung San hold that *n/um* (usually translated as 'spiritual energy' or 'potency') is stored in the pit of the stomach or base of the spine. The process of prolonged rhythmic dancing and singing, during their healing rituals, 'boils' the *n/um*, causing it to ascend up the body. The peak of the trance—full visionary conscious-ness, associated with soul-travel—is attained when the boiling *n/um* reaches the skull, inducing a state known as *!kia* (Gyrus 1998).

It would take truly awesome powers of difference-based thought to ignore the parallels! Yet the very similarities between these experiences, mediated via the tradi-tions of entirely different cultures, can be used to highlight the idiosyncrasies of each. For example, the !Kung *!kia* experience is brought about in a way that is communal and physically frenetic, and *!kia* itself is directly associated with active travel into visionary realms. Kundalini yoga is often a solo effort, practised by few in society. It does not normally involve much physical movement (except perhaps in sexual yogas), and the peak of the experience is seen to be one of blinding light or perceptual union with the environment. Traditional yoga frowns on the active participation in visionary realms. It is mysticism, not magic. These differences are of interest to the 'human sciences', looking at varied cultural responses to similar phenomena in human experience. An analysis of the differences between Kundalini yoga and !Kung trance practices will shed revealing light on the respective cultures they occur in (e.g. yogic non-attachment to, or avoidance of active visionary journeys may be related to the values of India's socio-religious structures, in contrast to those of the !Kung).

Difference and Similarity are related and complementary; each draws meaning from the other.

First-hand research

THE SIMILARITIES SEEM to be of more interest to those in the West practically engaged with the ranges of human consciousness—magicians, occultists, psychonauts, whatever you like to call such folk. The manifest parallels between different cultures' spiritual traditions are of interest to people who are attempting to recover a working relationship with these processes, within a culture which has lost all traditions dealing with such matters. Parallels may be used to try to uncover starting points, some 'baseline maps' of possibilities for human interaction with the more esoteric aspects of the body and environment. They may be also used to shed light on spontaneously occurring, often very unsettling experiences that cannot be usefully framed in Western paradigms.

The latter use of cross-cultural comparisons is precisely what has helped me, and many others in our culture, gain perspective on shattering personal experiences. Mine was a very disturbing experience with psychoactive chemicals, where I felt an 'essential force' rise up my body and threaten to burst out the top of my skull into a swirling vortex I saw in the sky. I felt like I was dying. Subsequently I learned—much to my relief—that there are other 'types' of dying that are not comprehended by our literal-minded, ecstasy-free culture.

Participatory interest in shamanism is, of course, responsible for much of the term's abuse. It also holds the key to a more sophisticated and—in the deepest sense of the word—scientific understanding of shamanism.

The abuses of the term in this area are largely to do with our own culture's lack of ecstatic religious traditions, and with our domination by consumerism. The first leads to a fragile or non-existent 'ecstatic cultural identity', hence a tendency to vampirize and distort other cultures. As the magician Phil Hine said in a recent interview, "I think we have to be very careful when we appropriate chunks of living magical traditions, otherwise it's Western imperialism all over again. The West has take their land, their culture, their dignity, and now we're coming back for their spiritual beliefs." (Gyrus 1998) The second factor here—consumerism—leads to distortions in popular perceptions of shamanism. The less marketable aspects of shamanism (e.g. torturous initiation rituals, genuine sorcery, a deep concern with death and dissolution) are naturally edged out of popular accounts and workshops sold to middle-class self-discoverers.

What were you on when you wrote that?

As far as the academic community is concerned, there is of course the strong suspicion of 'less than sober' modes of experience impinging on research. There has been a perpetual crisis on the fringes of academia since the 1960s around this issue, and it will simply have to come to terms with the full implications of altered states of consciousness (and thus consciousness itself) if it is to have any hope of remaining relevant to genuine human knowledge.

Recently, in *British Archaeology*, Paul Bahn made an oblique attack on the MA course in rock art at the University of Southampton, which is at the forefront of research into the interpretation of such art as a being related to shamanic activity. He sees such research—and specifically the idea that some rock art motifs may result from visions in altered states—as a "bandwagon … largely born of the drug age and the New Age phenomenon…" (Bahn 1998).

Bahn seems to think that those who take on board the shamanic hypothesis are excluding all other interpretative possibilities. In my view, they are merely redressing the balance. Not *every* study of rock art has to deal with *every* possibility; people are, by and large, astute enough to blend singular perspectives into the wider picture. And when one hugely important area of interpretation is lacking in the field, there is space for some specific focus on it, to fully drag it into the interpretative spectrum.

Incidentally, the independent researchers I know with extensive experience of psychedelics have been the first to point out holes in and exceptions to the theory of 'entoptic' geometric imagery influencing abstract glyphs in rock art. Actual experience of altered states, far from inducing a blinkered approach to theories about them, often leads to the most sophisticated approach (it's called knowing what you're talking about).

The fact is that Bahn is perceiving more 'shamanism-obsessed' research around him than there actually is (though he'd have a field-day with this essay). His accusations of projection and obsession merely reveal his own obsession with denouncing a new area of research. It is plain from his comment quoted above where the roots of his obsession lay: in the same soil that nourishes tabloid anti-drug hysteria, and the Thatcherite-Reaganite view that "it all went wrong in the sixties".

The Invisible College

HE IS RIGHT to be cynical about the 'New Age', but for the wrong reasons. In the eyes of someone like Bahn, the most intelligent, erudite and responsible modern student of psychedelic shamanism, totally unconcerned with the 'New Age', would fall into the same category as the flakiest, vaguest, fad-driven hippy. Naturally, people with little experience of Western subcultures end up not seeing past the images of drug culture, paganism and occultism that break through into the mainstream media. The Bahns of this world pose no threat at all to the 'unseen' (i.e. unmediated) explorers in this area—they will carry on regardless of popular perceptions. Indeed, their cultural 'invisibility' is in a way the core of their strength, as their research remains uncontaminated by mass-mediation, consumerism, and the vested interests of professional research. But the more conservative elements of academia do stand in the way of fruitful cross-fertilization between the cutting edge of academic research into shamanic altered states and participatory research into these areas. In other words, they block the development of an integrated approach to the exploration of first-hand spirituality, past and present.

Of course, it is only academia that can lose. As I said before, those of us who are personally (and not necessarily professionally) committed to rediscovering 'hands-on' religion will carry on regardless. And the barriers that often stop academics from reaping the benefits of 'knowing what you're talking about' are not there to stop occultists, pagans and users of psychedelics from drawing on academic research for a more balanced, integrated approach.

The Vortex

NEAR BOLTON ABBEY in West Yorkshire is a section of the River Wharfe called the Strid, where the current narrows down between rocks to form a foaming torrent. Folklore collected in late nineteenth century tells of a certain shadowy beast, known as a 'water kelpie', which may appear here (Bogg 1904a: 189).

This water fiend generally presented itself to the belated traveller in the shape of an old shaggy-haired pony near to some well-known crossing place on the bank of a river. But woe to the traveller who, to escape the discomfort of getting a wetting, unsuspiciously mounted the supposed steed! It instantly sprang with a wild shriek of laughter into the deepest whirlpool, without giving its human victim any chance of dismounting.

Bogg 1904b: 348

When I first read this passage, its 'shamanic' resonances immediately leaped out at me. I was well aware of the reasons why. Firstly, my experience of nearly being sucked into a vortex in the sky—which I had subsequently gained perspective on through researching shamanic experi-

The Strid gorge, West Yorkshire

ences—had led to a deep awareness of the association of vortex-like images with entry into otherworlds. The whirlpool is a good example of a naturally occurring vortex, and my research into shamanism had made me aware that shamans often use bodies of water as 'entrances' (see Halifax 1979: 61 for a !Kung example). I came to see the possibility that cup-and-ring motifs may be associated with this phenomenon about nine months before I learnt that respectable academics were also considering this—see Bradley 1997: 54.

Secondly, many years ago I had a dream in which I saw a brown horse pierced by a spear and fall to the ground. Then I was astride a winged white horse, flying up across the sea into the sky. Six months later I read Mircea Éliade's *Shamanism* for the first time, and was amazed to learn of a Siberian shamanic rite in which a horse is slain so that the shaman may enter the otherworld and use the horse's departed soul as a steed in that realm.

More recently, I was sent an article by Angelo Fossati dealing with Iron Age petroglyphs in Valcamonica, Italy (Fossati 1994). He discusses a depiction of a 'labyrinth', incorporating three human figures and a bird (right), relates examples in early European mythology of birds acting as guides for those entering

An Iron Age 'labyrinth' rock carving from the Naquane National Park, Val Camonica, Italy

the otherworld, and then details how the horse superseded the bird as the main guide of this type in European myth.

These elements—the vortex-entrance, and the horse as a ride/guide to the realms beyond it—resonated strongly for me with this little folktale of West Yorkshire. We may also note the liminal location of the water kelpie's appearance.

Does this mean I see it as a 'genuine' linear descendent of classical shamanic practices in the area? About as much as I take my various dreams and experiences as evidence for me being a shaman! I am interested here in what is usually known as the 'psychology' of myth. Psychologically speaking, I see the nature of this Yorkshire water kelpie as emanating from the same regions of human consciousness that are the focus of shamanic exploration. If nothing resembling the classical definition of 'shamanism' ever existed in Wharfedale (which I find hard to assert as an absolute statement), the origin of the water kelpie would be ascribed to local 'imagination'. Imagination was, in this case, probably put in the service of cautioning people, especially children, about the very physical dangers of this part of the Wharfe. But it is precisely this region—the human imagination—that is consciously entered, and explored in a spatially manifest form ('the otherworld') by the shaman. And I believe the imagination / otherworld is ultimately, if not wholly, non-local in nature.

Who's in control?

WE CAN SEE A FAILURE to understand the common underlying source of mythical and cultural artefacts in the rock art and shamanism controversy. Much of the debate centres around whether or not this or that motif was *directly* inspired by geometric hallucinations. But even if a certain motif was just 'imagined', and associated with things more mundane than altered states, it would still, by definition, owe its creation to the human imagination. Problems arise when we try to pinpoint the exact way in which a motif emerged from this pregnant realm—was it hauled out, or did it fall out?

Here we reach the key distinction between 'shamanic' and 'non-shamanic' motifs, in both art and myth: the former are *voluntarily* encountered and *actively* related to. The latter 'bubble up' into consciousness of their own accord, but frequently still resemble shamanic motifs in form, if not in the way humans relate to them. The water kelpie is an entity that is, according to the tale, 'misinterpreted' as a real animal, and seems to possess a slightly demonic, malevolent nature. To me, this demonstrates a manifestation of a common shamanic phenomenon that (1) is initially taken to be 'real' because it is not encountered voluntarily, with awareness, and (2) seems to be beyond control and malevolent because, again, it is not approached with conscious intention.

Again, it matters little to the 'psychological' view whether anyone ever "actually" encountered a water kelpie, voluntarily or otherwise, or whether the beast is a simple 'nursery bogie' used to warn children of the river's physical dangers. The *form* of the tale, even if it never ventured outside the human brain (which seems unlikely), still reveals the way in which shamanism can reflect the mind's methods of organizing imaginative / mythical reality.

The *voluntary* nature of shamanic activity is stressed to distinguish it from mere mental breakdown. And indeed, modern magic also stresses that 'intention is the key'. But, as any shrewd anthropologist or practising magician knows, human brushes with the otherworld are a little more complex. It appears to me, from my research into traditional shamanism, that intention and control are often factors that only come to the fore during and after shamanic training, or in formalized rituals. A shaman's initiation is frequently terrifyingly *out of control*. The otherworld initially bursts *into* the human world, not vice versa. The experience is only directed away from the anchor-less processes of schizophrenia by cultural convention and recognition of shamanic potentiality, ripe for training.

And I find it hard to believe that all shamans reach a point of total 'control' over their universe. They may stress their personal power as part of their method, or to induce faith in the people they heal, but I like to bear in mind the words of Huichol shaman Don José Matsúwa:

> *The shaman's path is unending. I am an old, old man and still a* nunutsi *[baby] standing before the mystery of the world.*

Schultes & Hofmann 1992: 138

Modern magicians are also coming to recognise the limits of control over the world:

> *Magick is defined as: causing change to occur in conformity with will, expanding your achievable reality, the pursuit of power, and so on. All these definitions presuppose control as the central theme in magick. This is all fine and good, but it illustrates that magick cannot address issues outside of the sphere of control. These are issues that are usually chunked up into mysticism ... This is a mistake, because half of our quality of experience is dependent on our ability to let go, stop worrying, stop controlling and enjoy. ... Therefore, magick can be seen as the pursuit of power, via the dynamic tension between ecstasy and control.*

Lee 1997: 13-15

I strongly suspect that most shamans would concur with such a view, if we get behind their professional bravado, and the cultural differences in our ways of mediating power, ecstasy and control.

We can see the control/ecstasy polarity in our comparison between !Kung trances and Kundalini yoga. The first is seen as 'shamanic/magical', the second as 'mystical'. This is a useful distinction on one level; but does it mean that !Kung medicine men never experience the free-flow ecstasy of the Indian Tantrika? I feel it merely means that !Kung social structure, incorporating fully communal, actively shamanic ceremonies, allows the experience of 'uncontrolled' ecstasy to be subtly blended into the very fabric of their shamanic experiences. It is not compartmentalized and placed on a pedestal, as in much 'mysticism'. As Lee says, "Control is the basis of magickal structures, defining one's will in a given situation, but without ecstasy it doesn't go. Without a tank full of gnosis, the magickal vehicle will not run." (*ibid.*: 14)

So, the issue of control in shamanism is not as clear-cut as some accounts imply. In contemporary society, we know from the testimony of many individuals (and I know from personal experience) that involuntary experiences of the otherworld do not necessarily lead to mental illness, as definitions of shamanism often presume. Whatever ontological validity you ascribe to reports of 'abduction by aliens', they are clearly as real to many of the people who experience them as a traditional shaman's journeys are to him or her. And again, they derive from the same regions of consciousness.

Patrick Harpur (1994) has made convincing comparisons between tribal puberty initiations, spontaneous shamanic initiation in the otherworld, and modern accounts of 'UFO abductions'. These frequently share a similar structure:

- isolation from community/'reality';
- the infliction of pain and possibly bodily mutilation;
- the transmission of esoteric knowledge to the initiate, shaman or 'abductee';
- and return to a world that is never quite the same again!

'Abductees' often have no knowledge of shamanism, and no history of 'mental illness'. Yet the parallels are astounding.

I once interviewed a woman (Gyrus 1995) who described her experience of smoking the potent hallucinogen dimethyltryptamine (used by many indigenous shamans in various organic forms). She was "grabbed" out of her initial experiences on the trip by an unseen force, and "landed in this dimension, and I wasn't free, I wasn't able to control where I went." Conveyed into the middle of a "grid-like structure", she was then reassured by an unmanifest "male entity". Told that she would find the following events frightening, but also that it would all be good for her, she proceeded to have each limb, one by one, ripped off and replaced. While each limb was off, "all this stuff ran out... I felt all my troubles, my aches and pains, my paranoias, come out." Then she "felt this mad feeling again, going up through my little toe, and it crawled all the way up my leg, and up through my body, and it felt like when it hit my heart, there was a massive explosion ... I've just never felt so amazing in my life. It felt like a complete cleansing process." Needless to say, she felt healthier, happier, and more psychically potent than ever for months to come! I asked her later if she had read anything about shamanism before this experience, and she hadn't; it was only afterwards that she encountered anthropological literature on the subject, which helped her understand her trip. Evidently there's something unprecedented and very interesting going on here, something touching deep levels of human consciousness.

The inter-disciplinary parallels I've drawn here are obviously just the tip of the iceberg. For those committed to the rigorous slicing-up of life for the purposes of a professional career in gaining and dispensing knowledge, the weight of these parallels can be a cumbersome burden; hence they are rarely even picked up. Those interested in all aspects of human experience need to be careful when confronted with such parallels, as they can lead into an interminable maze of intellectual associations. The way out of this maze is to discover the paradoxically idiosyncratic *and* universal nature of direct spiritual experience. Through this we can see, first-hand, just how Difference and Similarity gain there meaning from each other.

We always need to remember what 'shamanism' really is. *It is a modern Western conceptual construct, developed out of comparative anthropology.* In our discussions, we shouldn't forget that we define it, and are therefore at liberty to redefine it to suit the purposes of whatever form of research we are undertaking. Surviving indigenous 'shamanic' traditions will continue interacting with spirits in their own ways, whatever arguments transpire in academia about how a certain Siberian word may apply to them; modern magicians (and unsuspecting non-magicians) will do likewise.

Look again at Walsh's definition of shamanism, quoted near the start of this essay. In that form, it could easily apply to newly emerging traditions in Western society (with possible complexities around the definition of 'serving the community'—we have no unified 'community', so this definition will, for us, always be subject to mutation and debate). Also, note that Éliade's definition of shamanism can lead to the misleading idea that most young people in Britain are involved in this tradition every Friday night!

Very few modern magicians define themselves as 'shamans', simply because they are acutely aware of the historical and socio-cultural background to the term. However, they know that there is some inner congruence between their own activities and those of shamans throughout the ages, as there is between shamanic motifs and an amazing variety of human mythical constructs.

As a rough rule of thumb, I see the following distinctions in terminology:

shaman: A specific term that can only be validly applied to individuals within indigenous traditions

shamanism: A Western construct used to reflect the astounding parallels between such traditions across the globe, and presumably throughout history

shamanic: An adjective that may be used to draw attention to elements of myth, folklore, art, and hypothesized or actual spiritual activity that can be associated with motifs found in shamanism

Emphasis on diversity must not become a new monolithic creed in our awareness of ourselves. I feel it must be balanced against the somewhat unfashionable idea of a unity underlying human consciousness. The 'bathwater' in this idea is its rigidity, its lack of feel for multiplicity; the 'baby' is our common human *axis mundi*. Let's not throw away our own centre.

References

Bahn, P., 1998. 'Stumbling in the footsteps of St Thomas', *British Archaeology* no. 31, p. 18.

Bogg, E., 1904a, *Higher Wharfedale*, Petty & Sons.

— 1904b, *Lower Wharfedale,* James Miles.

Bradley, R., 1997, *Rock Art and the Prehistory of Atlantic Europe*, Routledge.

Éliade, M., 1989, *Shamanism: Archaic Techniques of Ecstasy*, Arkana.

Fossati, A., 1994, 'L'acqua, le armi el gli uccelli nell'arte rupestre camuna dell'età del Ferro', *Notizie Archeologiche Bergomensi* no. 2, pp. 203-216

Gyrus, 1995, 'Amy's DMT Trip', http://dreamflesh.com/interviews/amydmt/

— 1998, 'The San & the Eland', *Towards 2012* part 4, The Unlimited Dream Company.

— 1998, 'An Interview with Phil Hine', *Towards 2012* part 4, The Unlimited Dream Company.

Halifax, J., 1979, *Shamanic Voices: the Shaman as Seer, Poet and Healer*, Penguin.

Harpur, P., 1994, *Daimonic Reality: A Field Guide to the Otherworld*, Viking.

Lee, D., 1997, *Chaotopia! Magick & Ecstasy in the PandaemonAeon*, Attractor.

Mookerjee, A. & Khanna, M., 1977. *The Tantric Way*, Thames and Hudson.

Schultes, R.E. & Hofmann, A., 1992, *Plants of the Gods: Their Sacred, Healing and Hallucinogenic Powers*, Healing Arts Press.

Walsh, R.N., 1990. *The Spirit of Shamanism*, Mandala.

FORM & MEANING IN ALTERED STATES & ROCK ART

This was published in 1999 in the final issue of The Ley Hunter *(no. 133).*

Rock art has recently begun to cause more than a little conflict in academic archaeology. Curiously, the controversial discovery that some rock art was inspired by what we call 'shamanism' and 'altered states' was made through the dogged pursuit of scientific method, not through 'fringe' research. But as these areas brush against some of the deepest levels of the human psyche, they have inevitably raised a few hackles.

While not made in reference to these aspects of rock art, Richard Bradley's comment that rock art research "must contribute directly to archaeology if it is to achieve anything of value" (Bradley 1997: 8) is interesting. Evidently archaeologists are eager to keep their 'sub-discipline' firmly in their grasp. It can't help to have bugbears such as shamanism and altered states arriving on the scene. The first is a classic example of a multi-disciplinary phenomenon, due to it being essentially 'pre-disciplinary'. The latter, more often than not, utterly transcends such conceptual categories. Gradually, more and more respectable archaeologists, like Bradley, are paying heed to the 'trance interpretation' of rock art. But perhaps there is a lingering fear that the act of studying altered states and shamanism will influence those doing the studying, as it has in areas such as anthropology and psychology. Such influences may begin to dangerously loosen the boundaries of archaeology—boundaries that have been diligently erected in archaeology's long struggle to gain the status of being a 'science'...

A Trojan Horse?

THE 'ENTOPTICS'[1] THEORY of geometric rock art arose from comparisons between motifs in petroglyphs and hard neuroscience data about the 'form constants' that various altered states of consciousness can gener-ate in the visual field. But however much the theory was smothered in references to neurological studies, and decorated with reassuring graphs and tables, it carried with it the unmistakable whiff of non-ordinary consciousness. For perhaps the first time, this phenomenon could confidently raise its head in archaeology as well as anthropology, neuroscience and psychology departments. Not the romanticised magic associated with prehistory by early antiquarians; not the megalithic astronomy described by Profes-

ENTOPTIC PHENOMENA		
	A	B
I		
II		
III		
IV		
V		
VI		

sor Thom; not even the communal experience of formalised ritual. All these have been dismissed or absorbed by archaeology with relative ease. But the personal experience of losing contact with consensus reality and entering a wholly Other world raises too many questions and, let's face it, fears. Can we really grapple with this sort of subjectiv-ity when envisioning the distant past?

Altered states can not only shed light on the origin of form in some rock art; they can assist in assessing the possible significance of all rock art. Altered states radically affect our apprehension of meaning, and help considerably in expanding our capacity for modes of signification that are less linear, monolithic and immutable than the tradi-tions Western thought has inherited. Thus, worked with sensitively, they may provide keys to unlocking symbolic possibilities in prehistoric art and architecture—even if these relics' only connection to 'altered states' is the fact that they were created by

1. Championed by David Lewis-Williams and Thomas Dowson. 'Entoptic' literally means 'inner eye'.

cultures whose entire mindset was constantly 'altered', in relation to our own.

Models of trance

TO BEGIN WITH, we must look at the distinctions made in the 'pure' trance theory of rock art. 'Entoptic' images are generally understood to be abstract geometrical images (lines, dots, dashes, circles, spirals) that arise in the early stages of a trip to the otherworld.[2] 'Endogenous visual phenomena' are entoptics whose forms are seen to specifically arise from neural structures, especially those of the optical nerves.

This preliminary arena of geometrical imagery should be familiar to all with even mild experience of altered states. The literature associated with dimethyltryptamine (DMT) seems particularly relevant here. Although DMT occurs in many plants with a history of shamanic usage, and even occurs naturally in the human brain (Most 1986), it is usually used in the West in its smokeable synthesised form. When smoked, one immediately feels its effects; within a minute or two one reaches the peak of the trip. And one returns to 'normal' consciousness after about 15-20 minutes. The astonishingly rapid action of this compound means that the various stages of trance are tightly compressed, and are thus made clearer for explanatory purposes. Building on extensive accounts of various people's experiences, Peter Meyer (1994; a study that doesn't discuss rock art) breaks the DMT trip into levels, which may be used to model many similar forms of trance:

Level I: Pre-hallucinatory experience: This stage is characterized by an interior flowing of energy/consciousness.

Level II: Vivid, brilliantly coloured, geometric visual hallucinations: Here one is observing a patterned field, basically two-dimensional, although it may have a pulsating quality. One may remember having seen this before.

Transitional Phase (Level IIB?): tunnel or breakthrough experience: One may see or fly through a tunnel... A veil may part, a membrane may be rent. There is a breakthrough to another world (or perhaps even a series of breakthroughs). Alternatively, it may happen that the transition from Level II to Level III is abrupt, almost instantaneous, with no experience of transition.

Level III: Three- or higher-dimensional space, possible contact with entities: This

---

2. I like the term 'otherworld', despite its neo-Celtic connotations. To me it simply signifies a self-consistent world that is Other than this one, only accessible via altered states. Its after-death connotations are, given shamanic testimony, entirely appropriate.

stage is characterized by the experience of being in an "objective" space, that is, a space of at least three dimensions in which objects or entities may be encountered. Sometimes the entities appear to be intelligent and communicating beings.

Level II is the arena of entoptic imagery, and is the prime concern of rock art researchers looking at abstract geometrical shapes. It is these forms that are posited as being transcultural, arising from the very structures of the human nervous system. The 'transitional' phase also enters this arena in rock art studies. Bradley (1997) associates the concentric circular patterns in cup-and-ring art with tunnel-like images common to entry into profound altered states; Dronfield (1996) associates these images with both the tunnel-like entrances and the spiral art found in passage graves in Ireland.

Level III is what I call 'full visionary consciousness', and can relate to rock art that depicts representative forms (e.g. therioanthropic images). This level is seen by most rock art researchers to be culture-bound. That is, the forms of entities (spirits, gods, ancestors) encountered here—and the transformed identity of the voyager—are clothed with culturally-defined expectations. Thus, for example, an Amazonian *ayahuasquero*'s[3] Level III may be replete with jaguars and anacondas, while a San medicine man's Level III may be clothed with antelope and giraffe.

An obvious question, though, is whether a San person taken to the Amazon to partake of an *ayahuasca* ritual will still find the otherworld populated with African fauna. Are Level III's 'clothes' contained within the acculturated portions of a person's mind, or can they emerge from a highly transpersonal interaction with the immediate ecosystem? A friend visited the Amazon recently and, during an *ayahuasca* ceremony, saw, alongside angels from his Catholic upbringing, a very unusual animal he had never encountered before. Days later he saw this otherworld animal's real counterpart in the jungle. Suffice it to say that Level III is much too vast a can of worms to really prise open here.

Narrow visions

I've only come across one archaeologist who has busied himself inordinately with dismissing the 'trance theory' area of research. In *British Archaeology*, Paul Bahn wrote an article called 'Stumbling in the footsteps of St Thomas' (1998). He compared

3. An *ayahuasquero* is a shaman whose sacramental psychedelic is the potent brew called *ayahuasca*. This comprises varying hallucinogenic plants, usually DMT-containing varieties, plus the harmine-containing *Banisteriopsis* vine.

the rise in attempts to interpret prehistoric rock art in terms of shamanic altered states to 16th century Christian missionaries who attributed 'footprints' in South American rock art to St Thomas. This analogy was in fact a thinly disguised attack on the students of the MA in rock art at Southampton University, which was devised by Thomas Dowson (the analogy also insinuates a degree of hoodwinking in Dowson's teaching methods). The students on this course responded to the attack, and in his reply to this Bahn said that his article had brought much congratulatory feedback, and that the only negative response was from the students in question. Nevertheless, the only response to the article printed in *British Archaeology* (not from one of the students in question) rightly criticised Bahn for universally dismissing the 'shamanic hypothesis' (Chapman 1998). And in the commentaries on Dronfield's article in the *Cambridge Archaeological Journal*, from a variety of experts in the field, Bahn stands alone in his dismissal of altered states.

Bahn appears to be quite isolated in his opposition to this field of study, and criticism of his reactionary views may appear redundant. However, his biases are no doubt shared by many other less public voices, and a close examination of what they represent should prove useful in divining and breaking down restrictive attitudes to rock art and altered states in general.

Firstly, it must be said that his main point of criticism is actually based on important perceptions:

> *Interpretations in rock art studies—and indeed in archaeology as a whole—come in cycles or phases that often reflect their period and cultural background. Hence Lerio-Gourhan's binary and sexual approach was born of the French structuralism and the sexual revolution of the 1950s and 1960s, and the astronomical approach came into its own during the Space Age. The current paradigm, trend, fad or bandwagon—as one might call it depending on where one's own sympathies lie—seems to be the direct legacy of the drug culture of the late 1960s and 1970s, with its attendant interest in mysticism and shamanism, hallucinogens, altered states of consciousness, etc., all of which have coalesced into the massive 'New Age' literature of the 1980s and 1990s.*

> Paul Bahn (in Dronfield 1996)

Some crucial distinctions need to be made in this inaccurate morass of classification, if we are to clearly understand the cultural juncture we stand at which has made academic contemplation of theories about phenomena such as entoptics possible.

His use of the term 'New Age' implies an awareness of this field not very far removed from that of the average tabloid reader. The social phenomenon that *calls itself* 'New Age' is not really concerned with hallucinogens and authentic shamanism. The "drug culture of the late 1960s and 1970s" has *not* coalesced into the 'New Age'. A diversification has occurred, leaving the more fad-driven factions in the public eye. However, far below the cultural horizons of *Daily Express* readers thrives a bunch of serious researchers concerned with psychedelic shamanism (see works by Terence McKenna, Jonathon Ott & Jim de Korne) and altered states in ritual (see works by Dave Lee, Phil Hine & Jan Fries).

But all this solid exploration would be neither here nor there to those who see it as some backwash from the sixties. To these people, interest in altered states is merely a decadent and temporary fad, which we'll probably all 'grow out of' sooner or later. Just like the Amazonian *ayahuasqueros*, Mexican *curanderos*, Indian tantrikas, African Bwiti cultists and San medicine men, Siberian and Eskimo shamans, Haitian voudon priests, Australian Aborigines, Nepalese sorcerors, Hawaiian Huna healers, Huichol Indians, and Native Americans, I suppose.

The dismissal of the "cycles" of archaeological theory as 'fads' amounts to a misperception of the way we are gradually recovering awareness of our environment and experience. Professor Thom's megalithic astronomy theories may well have been made possible by the cultural milieu of the Space Age; but they uncovered a vital aspect of megalithic culture that now has a firm place in the archaeologist's collection of lenses with which to view prehistory. The "'shamanism' bandwagon" we are now "suffering" (Bahn 1998) is neither a bandwagon nor something to wake up screaming about—unless of course your ego structures are so rigid that they view challenges such as altered states with abject terror. No—it is a recovery of awareness.

Interpretations old & new

I HAVE BEGUN to take a shine to the view that all cultures have 'interpreted' art and monuments left by previous cultures. And yes, each interpretation says as much about the interpreting culture as the originators. Medieval peasants often 'interpreted' prehistoric cup-marks as places to make libations to elemental spirits (see Bennett 1998). The clergy from the same period had very different ideas about such relics, usually involving Satan and his little wizards. Interpretations in the twentieth century have chopped and changed as rapidly as Western culture in this period. But there is a vital distinction to be made between the interpretations of country folk up into living memory, and those made by academic researchers. Pre-twentieth century rustics, unlike most rock art researchers, *still retained the archaic feeling that the land is alive with spirit.* And, most importantly, they used and interacted with these remnants of cultures long gone.

Most academics, in looking at the "cycles" of modern interpretation, neglect the larger picture. Our current view of archaic art reflects our alienated paradigm, wherein we study the environment in an uninvolved way, never thinking to *interact* with it. In this sense, there is a much larger gulf between medieval peasants and us than there is between

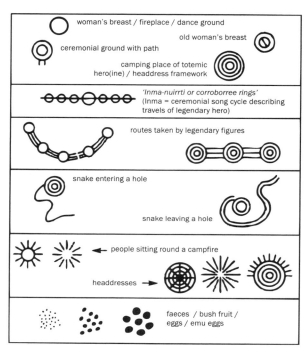

woman's breast / fireplace / dance ground

ceremonial ground with path

old woman's breast

camping place of totemic
hero(ine) / headdress framework

'Inma-nuirrti or corroborree rings'
(Inma = ceremonial song cycle describing
travels of legendary hero)

routes taken by legendary figures

snake entering a hole

snake leaving a hole

people sitting round a campfire

headdresses →

faeces / bush fruit /
eggs / emu eggs

Various meanings ascribed to circular forms in aboriginal Australian art by aboriginal informants. From information collected over the past 100 years from across the continent (after Layton 1992).

medieval peasants and their Neolithic ancestors. I fully recognise the difficulties in using folklore collected over the past two hundred years to gain ideas about the original purpose of prehistoric carvings and monuments; but even if the specifics are wide of the mark, the essential perception that nature is alive, and bursting with sentience, brings us much closer to understanding these relics than any quantifiable, measurement-based fieldwork.

Another interesting aspect of Bahn's attack is that he cites our obvious inability to "be sure" what rock art motifs were intended to represent as an argument against the 'trance vision' interpretation. All I can say is that a human whose vision is only interested in what can be known with absolute certainty is hideously impoverished. Bahn says that "one of the joys of prehistoric art is that it does not necessarily require interpretation, and can convey huge amounts of information of other kinds—in its technology (including pigment analyses), in its location, … and in its dating." (1998)

Joys?! In the end it's each to their own—but I'd rather not limit myself to such meagre data purely because it's a 'safe bet'. That isn't to dismiss the essential work in the arenas mentioned; it's just to say that a timid self-restriction to these 'certainties' cannot hope to fulfil healthy human curiosity and need for meaning.

Multiple meanings

WE'LL NEVER DECISIVELY nail down the significance of prehistoric rock art, obviously. But why should we not try to unfold the many possible meanings, and let them exist untethered? This may broaden our vistas of past art, and perhaps of present and future art, too. Indeed, much ethnographic evidence (e.g. Layton's study of Aboriginal art, 1992) suggests that preliterate artists never even *intend* that elusive singular 'meaning', the certainty that scientistic researchers vainly lust for. Abstract symbols such as Aboriginal concentric circles or European cup-and-rings are obviously amenable to polysemy, the existence of many meanings. In Australia we have clear ethnographic accounts to help us in interpretation; in Europe we have scant folklore (though this may often be useful, as I have already mentioned). But even if we cannot safely ascribe Aboriginal meanings to cup-and-rings here, we can at least appreciate the importance of polysemy in preliterate signification—and realise that we can neither nail singular meanings to our prehistoric art nor shy away, in reactionary fear, from attempts to raise plausible possibilities.

A linguistic example of polysemy, which may show how alien *singular* meanings are to many non-Western cultures, occurs in relation to petroglyphs in Hawaii. At Puuloa, a large hill of solidified lava, there is testimony from the nearest inhabitants that cup-marks are used when a child is born (Cox & Stasack, 1970). They translate 'Puuloa' as meaning 'Hill of Long Life'; when a baby is born, they go there to carve a new cup. They place the baby's

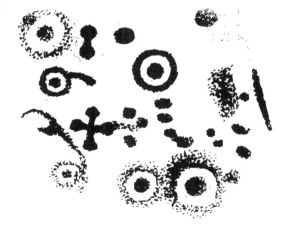

Petroglyphs from Puuloa, Hawaii
(after Cox & Stasack 1970).

piko—which may mean 'umbilical stump' or 'umbilical cord'—in it, cover it with a stone, and leave it overnight. "If the *piko* remained overnight (or disappeared—there is conflicting evidence about which would be effective) long life would be assured for the child." (*ibid.*) But *piko* is not limited to only two possible meanings:

> *As a noun it refers to the navel, navel string, and umbilical cord. Figuratively it can be used to refer to a blood relative and also to the genitals. It can be used to describe the summit of a hill, the crown of the head, tip of the ear, end of a rope, and the place where a leaf is attached to the stem. There are many other meanings, as is the case with very many Hawaiian words.*

> (*ibid.*)

Polysemy reveals a richness of signification that has become more and more alien to us since monotheistic literalism and the codification of language represented by dictionaries. The associations that polysemy weaves between different ideas and forms—wonderfully evident in the above example—allow for a perception of the world that owes more to the self-similar hierarchies of fractal theory than to the cut-and-dried isolation of meaning inherent in the Western rationalist paradigm.

But how in hell do you know what someone's going on about with this many possibilities? In short: the ambiguities of communication are ironed out with context—either surrounding words and symbols, or, more interestingly, *bodily presence*. In using language that can refer to many things, it is vocal tonality, and the silent expression of gesture, eye contact and generalised 'body language' that steers verbal vehicles of expression:

> *In more traditional worlds … I've noticed that people remain much more attuned to the languages of gesture; where there's no TV & "nothing ever happens", people watch people, people read people… I never knew this till I lived in Asia. Here in America, people react to you most often on the basis of the idea you project—thru clothes, position (job), spoken language. In the East one is more often surprised to find the interlocutor reacting to an inner state; perhaps one was not even aware of this state, or perhaps the effect seems like "telepathy". Most often, it is an effect of body language.*

> Hakim Bey

Here we need to appreciate the subtleties implied in the term 'altered state'. It needn't necessarily imply a wild trance, a voyage into the otherworld. A native of Darjeeling, in relation to our 'normal' consciousness, is in a constantly 'altered state'. Culture is a drug—and each variant has its own nuances, induces differing sensitivities to environmental cues and sensory stimuli. We rarely notice that we're loaded on culture because most people around us are too. This awareness of 'altered states' needs to be applied to signification in prehistoric art—to realise that these carvings were originally perceived from a totally different standpoint to ours, even by 'passers-by'.

Transcending the borders of sense

OUR UNDERSTANDING OF POLYSEMY may also be fruitfully enhanced by more intense altered states. Most interesting of all are experiences of synaesthesia (most common when using potent psychedelics), where signification becomes a complex trans-sensory experience that far surpasses frozen words. Polysemy is no longer: "This thing here may refer to that, that, or that"—because the extra dimensions and dynamic nuances involved in psychedelic spaces allow a transcendence of the linearity of language, and the 'piecemeal' signification it involves.

Clearly, some form of mutually agreed-upon system of signification is still needed to understand symbols arranged in such a space; but a right-brained task like this may well be simpler for 'preliterate' cultures than for our own, just as it is often simpler for someone who is stoned on tryptamines than for someone who isn't. Terence McKenna's fieldwork in the Amazon has convinced him that the "magical songs of the *ayahuasqueros*, the folk *medicos* of the Indians and mestizos of the jungle back rivers, are not song as we understand the term. Rather they are intended to be seen and to be judged primarily as visual works of art. To those intoxicated and adrift upon the visionary reveries unleashed by the brew, the singing voice of the shaman has become a magical airbrush of color and organized imagery that is breathtaking in its alien and cosmic grandeur." (McKenna 1991)

A mild experience of such synaesthesia once opened me up to new possibilities in rock art. Having taken some 2CB (a synthetic phenethylamine), I went to the Badger Stone on Ilkley Moor to experiment with harmonic chanting. I put my face about 5 inches from a bare, uncarved surface and began chanting. I kept my eyes open. What occurred was a meshing of entoptic phenomena (usually assumed to manifest behind closed eyelids) and exterior reality—in this case the plain rock surface.

But it isn't 'plain' at all. It is alive with the tiny crystalline structures that compose the rock surface itself. There's no 'blank canvas' in rock art! As I chanted, the irregular pattern of these crystals smoothly coalesced into a regular lattice-work pattern, always gently shifting. Embedded in this lattice were diaphanous symbols—the usual lines and circles, again always mutating. Their form and movement appeared to correspond

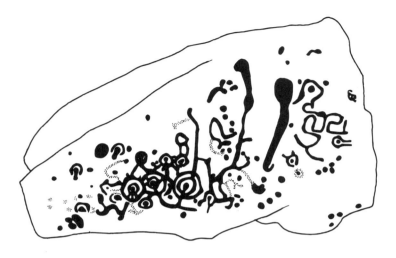

Carvings on the Badger Stone (after Hedges 1986).

to the modulation of my voice.

As I hit a certain tone, the patterns seemed to reach a certain stability, and the atmosphere was charged with a pregnant and slightly ominous expectation. Nothing dramatic followed. But my feeling was that if I had taken a slightly larger dose, or perhaps if I had managed to side-step the familiar shock that impending tears in the fabric of reality induce, I would have gone *into* the rock.

This reminded me of an article I had read:

> *In many cultures, the shaman in his trance passes through the rock into the spirit world, and to communicate what had happened in the trance, the shaman depicts what had happened on the other side on the rock... In addition, several contemporary shamans have acknowledged that the rock art is a marker for where a shaman could enter the rock.*

Grant S. McCall

Could vocally-induced altered states, perhaps aided by other trance induction methods, have played a part in the genesis of some rock art? There is strong evidence that acoustic effects such as echoes play a part in the Korku tribe's decisions for locating rock paintings, and Steven Waller has found unusual echoes at over 100 rock art sites across the globe (Trubshaw 1997). Whether this idea can be extended to include the more intimate use of voice seen in my own experience is unclear; but the notion of entoptic phenomena being seen, not behind closed eyelids, but *on the rock surface itself*, is surely intriguing when considering rock art. Even more intriguing is the idea that the genesis of some prehistoric visual forms may have been rooted in synaesthetic experience, and owed as much to sonic performances as they did to purely 'visual' phenomena.

Transmedia contexts

WE SHOULD REALISE the full extent to which our division of 'the arts' into respective media—writing, song, dance, visual arts, etc.—may blind us to the function of rock art. The term 'multimedia' has recently narrowed in meaning to refer to shoving a CD into a computer. Perhaps we should adopt the term 'transmedia' to refer to attempts to break down the walls between various artistic media in an active, body-centred way (see P-Orridge, 1997). 'Transmedia' is to separate artistic media what synaesthesia is to the five senses; and both may inform our view of preliterate cultures.

Citing Nancy Munn's research into the teaching systems of Aboriginal mothers, where symbolic visual elements, hand gestures and language are utilised simultaneously to impart information about the mythical landscape, Robert Andreas Fischer (1997) argues:

> *So-called orality within indigenous societies has ... never existed. Oral communication is the tag non-alphabetical literate societies have received from alphabetic literate societies. In reality, so-called oral communication is composed of an extremely sophisticated, multi-layered, polysemic codification-system of simultaneous communication systems. The "orality" of indigenous societies is actually a form of "savage multi-mediality".*

We cannot let any trace of our 'frame & gallery' approach to visual art distort our investigations into carvings that were probably part of a culture where different artistic media flowed into each other, and merged with the environment.

> *In the archaic universe all things were signs and signatures of each other, inscribed in the hologram, to be divined subtly.*
>
> Giorgio de Santillana & Hertha von Dechend, *Hamlet's Mill*

IN UNEARTHING ROCK ART's many possible meanings, we must be cautious about saying that meanings 'belong' to such-and-such a painting or petroglyph. Especially when dealing with abstract symbols. For if we are to take the Aboriginal mothers' methods of teaching to be a viable contextual possibility for prehistoric rock art, we must consider the possible replication of the symbol in other media, and even in the environment.

What I mean by this can be seen if we visualise scenarios around, say, the Badger Stone. Perhaps some symbols on the stone are replicated in geoglyphs on the ground before it, or on body paintings or tattoos. It is impossible for those present to consider these symbols as wholly distinct from the bodily motions, ritual actions, vocal performances or stories woven around and among them. The symbols on the stone are *not* the foundation or 'base' of the web of significance; they are merely elements *in* the network. (But then the same is true of all symbols, even today—only the linearity of prose blinds us to this.)

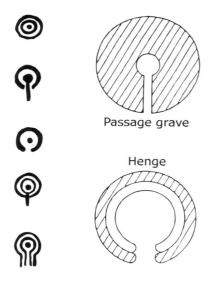

Passage grave

Henge

Similarities between the forms of cup-and-rings and monumental structures (after Trubshaw 1997).

This network extends outwards beyond human society. A cup-and-ring could relate to the form of a burial construction (see Bradley 1997), a water source, a heavenly body (e.g. the Pole Star—see Oakley 1998), a whirlpool, a tunnel to the otherworld, or the circle of the horizon. The network of meanings could also extend inwards beyond culture: to the eye, mouth, breast, nipple, navel, vagina, anus, or neural structure. Any or all of these references could coexist simultaneously in the web of meaning.

This vision of signification, with meanings floating in a complex pool of cross-references, where symbols are only anchored to human life through ritual and the body, is what I have been led to through my experiences of altered states and my study of rock art. It obviously presents a difficult challenge to Western academic traditions (be they institutionalised or not). The only language that can grapple with this vision is one that owes as much to poetry as to prose, and more to play than to work. And maintaining this vision requires something that breaks many boundaries of intellectual study: active involvement.

There is a huge amount of study to be done, and fun to be had, in interpreting and revitalising archaic artforms. We should not let the inherent uncertainty and multiplicity of meaning involved in this task discourage us; but rather appreciate and enjoy the many-faceted, unfixable nature of reality that makes these things inherent. Beyond entoptics, I feel that it is in the comprehension of this more general paradigm that altered states—both subtle and intense—will benefit rock art research.

A personal testament to the archetypal nature of vortex imagery. I did the finger-painting on the right after a psilocybin-fuelled Chemical Brothers gig, 7/10/95. Six months later the 5 year-old daughter of a friend spontaneously presented me with the drawing shown above.

References

Bahn, Paul, 1998, 'Stumbling in the footsteps of St Thomas' in *British Archaeology* February 1998

Bennett, Paul, 1998, 'Cup-and-Ring Art: Its Folklore, Myths, and the Shamanic Perspective' in *Towards 2012 part IV*, Unlimited Dream Company

Bey, Hakim, n.d., 'Evil Eye', http://www.spunk.org/texts/writers/bey/sp000536.html

Bradley, Richard, 1997, *Rock Art and the Prehistory of Atlantic Europe*, Routledge

Chapman, Bill, 1998, Letter in *British Archaeology* April 1998

Cox, J. Halley & Stasack, Edward, 1970, *Hawaiin Petroglyphs*, Bishop Museum Press

de Santillana, Giorgio & von Dechend, Hertha, 1999, *Hamlet's Mill: An Essay Investigating The Origins Of Human Knowledge And Its Transmission Through Myth*, Godine

Dronfield, Jeremy, 1996, 'Entering Alternative Realities: Cognition, Art and Architecture in Irish Passage-Tombs' in *Cambridge Archaeological Journal* vol. 6

Fischer, Robert Andreas, 1997, 'Protohistoric Roots of the Network Self' in *Towards 2012 part III*, Unlimited Dream Company

Hedges, John D. (ed.), 1986, *The Carved Rocks of Rombald's Moor*, West Yorkshire Archaeological Service

Layton, Robert, 1992, *Australian Rock Art: A New Synthesis*, Cambridge University Press

McCall, Grant S., n.d., 'One Medium, One Mind', http://www.geocities.com/Athens/Forum/3339/rockart.html

McKenna, Terence, 1991, *The Archaic Revival*, HarperSanFrancisco

Meyer, Peter, 1994, 'Apparent Communication with Discarnate Entities Induced by Dimethyltryptamine (DMT)' in Lyttle, Thomas (ed), *Psychedelics*, Barricade Books

Most, Albert, 1986, 'Eros & the Pineal', http://www.magnet.ch/serendipity/dmt/eros.html

Oakley, G.T., 1998, *Verbeia: The Goddess of Wharfedale*, Norlonto

P-Orridge, Genesis, 1997, 'Thee Splinter Test' in *Towards 2012 part III*, Unlimited Dream Company

Trubshaw, Bob, 1997, 'The Altering State of Rock Art Research' in *At The Edge* no. 8

AEONS PAST & PRESENT

This was written in 1998, originally intended for the final part of Towards 2012, *themed 'Apocalypse', and my intention was to use a simplistic model to summarise my ideas about time, history and evolution. As I thinned down my conceptions of this final part, focusing it on specifically apocalyptic ideas, this extensive piece was left to languish on my hard drive. Now I'm finally publishing it, of course it contains many points and ideas I'd probably not agree with now, but these things deserve to stand on their own feet, however aged… It should be mentioned that this predates by a long way my encounter with Ramsey Dukes' excellent elaborations of the Thelemic Aeonic model—collected in* What I Did In My Holidays *(Mandrake Press, 1998). Encountering these ideas at the time of writing this essay would no doubt have influenced things here a lot, and confused me greatly.*

O
UR EXPERIENCE OF THE WORLD is governed by many structures: our bodies, our emotions, our mental processes, our physical environments (natural and constructed), our cultures, our social circles… The most basic structures of existence seem to be those which encompass it all: *space and time.*

These are very broad terms that seem to refer to concrete 'things', namely our physical sense of place and movement, and our mental feeling of 'moving forwards' from one moment to another. But if we step for a while outside the habits of perception we've accumulated, we may see that space and time are actually malleable, mutable and extremely fluid. Any fixed idea of them is in fact an illusory construct—a false representation, a consensus belief which has hardened into an unconscious assumption, moulding our immediate experience from 'behind the scenes'.

Space and time are qualities of the world that manifest in different forms for different consciousnesses. The space and time of a dolphin is very different from that of a bat; both are very different from our space and time. Thus, when we say "space" and "time", we actually mean "human space" and "human time". Sometimes we may even mean "human English space/time" or "human London space/time"; often we mean "my space/time". Our perception of time has more to do with how we behave and how our bodies and minds are structured than it has to do with being an abstract, ever-lasting medium. Psychedelic drugs are a good indicator of how the experience of time is dependent on other factors. A minute addition to your body chemistry can do very drastic things to the idea that time is an untouchable, ever-forward-flowing medium that we pass through.

Space and time are, of course, seen in post-Einstein scientific terms, part of one space-time continuum. Space has come to be seen not as a vacant 'absence' in which 'things' move around, but as the very fabric in which material processes are embedded. Time, it seems, remains a much more mysterious aspect of this continuum. Space is fine—we can walk over to the park and walk back again, or even pop into the pub on the way. But time appears to be an intangible one-way street, an irreversible forwards flow over which we have little or no control.

Terence McKenna has described evolution as a progressive conquering of dimensions; from aimless floating about in the sea, to increasing mobility and control of the spatial environment, to our 'conceptual control' of time through writing and documentation. Despite this conceptual control, we still seem to experience time as a dimension that controls us, that carries us along to our deaths. It's this lack of control (and fear of death) that imbues time with such mystery, and stimulates our interest in figuring it all out.

There are many inspired quantum physicists who have been working for quite a while on breaking the apparent limitations of time down. But here I'm not going to be concerned with the science end of the spectrum. I want to look at the 'history of time', how cultures through the ages seem to have perceived time, and how these perspectives can help us model our different 'time trances'—our key modes of perceiving time in the present—and open up possibilities for the 'future of time'.

I'll mostly be talking about time and not space, despite their scientific unity. I think the constructs of time through which we perceive the world condition and limit so many aspects of our lives—actually, *all* of our lives—that they deserve special attention from those concerned with unwinding conditioning and dissolving limitations.

Time in the past

THE CENTRAL ASPECT of the study of time is the contrast between *abstract* and *experienced* time, between our *models* of time and our *feeling* of time. These two aspects of time will be referred to as 'measured time' and 'human time'.

Abstract calendars like our own give us a conceptual habit of visualizing time as a 'line'—*linear time*. Think of time-charts showing the past to the left, going forward in time to the right. Think of one for us humans, going back to the first ape flipping out up to the present moment.

Now think of the infinite complexity of the present world; the billions and billions of people out there with entirely different worldviews; the thousands of different overlapping cultures, many with radically different notions of time to yours; the unfathomable ranges of human consciousness going on out there, from ecstatic experiences of eternity to frustrated feelings of finitude and transience, from perspectives of dizzying freedom and complexity to painfully narrow experiences of senseless repetition and conformity; the different seasons (or lack of seasons) in different climates; all those people thinking "Shit!" as the alarm tells them it's time to trudge down to the factory, and all those people wandering home in the small hours, full of crystal-clear glee after an all-night party. Think of all this seething on the planet's surface, turning in on itself and then radiating out at impossible angles.

Now project the enormity of this bubbling vista back along that time-line; back beyond the point where people realized Earth was more than a few thousand years old; back beyond the point where people started writing and accumulating any idea of 'history' at all; way back, where our ideas of possible pasts multiply beyond number into a bewildering network of alternative time-lines radiating out from the present moment...

Evidently, linear time has the same bearing on reality as a CV has on personality. It's merely a crude indication, which inevitably distorts, and is only useful for really mundane stuff.

The model of history[1] I'll be using as a tool to open up different cans of worms in the study of time is an aeonic model that has emerged from chaos magic.[2] It has a

---

1. 'History' refers, of course, to written history. "What we call history is the history of the word." (Burroughs, *The Ticket That Exploded*) Periods before the invention of writing are referred to as 'prehistoric'. The cut-off point between history & prehistory cannot be dated in global terms—some cultures are still 'prehistoric'. For the West, written history begins around 5,000 years ago in Sumer. Sometimes I'll say 'history' & mean 'prehistory and history'—it should be obvious when this is the case.

2. Proposed by Peter J. Carroll in *Liber Null*, developed by Dave Lee in *Chaotopia!*; the model here is

linear element, and is extremely simplified, but its roots in a magical current immediately remind us that essentially it's a myth. It can be seen as a post-scientific mythical model of measured time, which is still relevant to human time in that it may also be made to refer to present modes of consciousness—*time trances*. Although it does relate to scientific models, its lack of 'scientific status' allows us enough space to see it as our own mythical construct of the past, of the 'inner levels of history'.

To explain: From one point of view, Australian Aboriginal Dreamtime myths, describing ancestor-beings roaming around the landscape forming and naming this waterhole and that hill, are distorted simplifications of complex geological processes that sculpted the continent's surface, and the activities of predecessors long lost in the past. From another viewpoint—the one we'll take here!—they are sophisticated and elegant stories that give humans, within their limitations, some intuitive comprehension of the land's past. These stories of the past also relate to the present. The myths form a deftly codified, usable navigational map for long walks (see Bruce Chatwin's excellent *The Songlines*). Also, the journeys and deeds of the ancestor-beings, and thus the landscape, underpin Aboriginal social organization and ritual activity.

My Aeonic model is not a story in the same sense as Dreamtime myths; but it is a story, and an elegant one, for those who have come out the other side of Science and seen the essentially fictional nature of culture's version of reality. More importantly, it's accessible. Although it becomes richer in meaning (and more obviously simplified and 'mythical') the more you learn about history, you don't have to spend all your spare time studying history to grasp it.

To compare again with Aboriginal culture, it has to be remembered that Aborigines (at least until Europeans and alcohol arrived) put as much energy, if not more, into understanding their Dreamtime as academics put into understanding 'history'. But tribal understanding flows through art, ritual and social life, not through intellectual research. Their understanding of the past is firmly entwined with their present, the very activities that sustain their social, emotional and spiritual energies.

Intellectual study—whether as part of academic institutions or outside them—is our only consciously codified tradition of understanding the past, and unfortunately it often amounts to an alienation from the present. There is a place for models of understanding that align more easily with the chaotic nature of our culture.

---

based on Lee's version, and is further inspired by Antero Alli's 'Neuropharmacology of an Eight-Circuit Brain' (http://dreamflesh.com/essays/neuropharm/).

My Aeonic model

THIS IS A ROUGH ILLUSTRATION of the model, showing the bindu-like 'Zero Aeon' in the centre, surrounded by the Five Aeons, and transcended by the Pandaemonaeon.

While the model is designed to emphasise non-linearity, there is a flow which corresponds to our conception of linear history, moving from the First Aeon (roughly corresponding to the lunar-based Palaeolithic), to the Second Aeon (the solar-based Neolithic and metal ages), to the Third Aeon (the historical monotheisms), to the Fourth Aeon (science and imperialism), to the Fifth Aeon—current chaos. The inadequacies and resonances of this linear path will be explored fully; for now it's sufficient to grasp its basics.

While looking at the Five Aeon model, a common reaction among magicians and pagans will be to map the five Aeons onto the traditional five elements. The First might be water, due to its oceanic communal ecstasies and association with lunar/menstrual rhythms. The Second, fire: agricultural concern with the sun and the 'heat' of fertility. The Third, air: abstraction and the over-valuation of the intellect. The Fourth, earth: materialism, everything understood in literal terms. The Fifth, spirit: more than the sum of the rest, containing all possibilities.

This is all a little forced, though, as are most correspondences. For instance, the Second Aeon's concern with agriculture could well associate it with earth rather than fire. But it reminds us that the model can be seen to refer to modes of experience as well as periods in the past. It is only through apprehending the Aeons as mythical models of present experience—represented in the form of our stories about the past—that we can undercut the illusion that our present culture is some sort of pinnacle of development. I've arranged the Aeons in the diagram in a roughly pentagonal fashion to remind us of their magical, non-linear underpinnings. I've also used a so-called 'inverse' pentagonal arrangement, again too undercut the 'pinnacle' illusion.

It should be stressed that it is essentially a myth for post-industrial societies. I'll mostly be referring to the evolution of cultures in Europe that have culminated in our post-colonial Western technocracy (though I'll draw on other cultures to highlight our losses and to keep in mind the multiplicity and non-linearity of our species). The narratives I'll dish out are Eurocentric in terms of history—but not in terms of prejudice or value-judgement. It's not intended to exclude other cultures, but to understand our own. It only makes sense in linear, 'progressive' terms when seen from the point of view of post-industrial culture.

However, no 'progress' is assumed—quite the opposite. Being told from the point of view of a contemporary magical current, it is biased in seeing a 'downward' trend in history, away from ecstasy and magic. There is an eventual 'return', giving it a cyclic flavour. If one chooses to relate it, as I will, to the archaeological record, its apparently linear structure breaks down into Aeonic overlaps and fractals. The Aeons bleed into each other. Even today, there are some people in the British Isles whose lives have more in common with the Second Aeon than the Fifth. And despite the onslaught of Western imperialism, there are still people in the world today living very much in the First Aeon. When we try to view the Aeons historically, such overlaps and interweaving is evident throughout. Again, the strictly linear element is only part of the picture, and is itself a way of mythologizing the West's descent into profane time and loss of ecstasy.

Today, many people brought up in Fifth Aeon cultures have reverted to a pseudo-Second or even pseudo-First Aeon existence. Of course, this is one of the features of the current Fifth Aeon: it is where history begins to 'open up' and allow elements of 'past' Aeons into the present, blending different Aeonic tendencies and creating ever more hybrid Aeonic styles. In chaos magic theory, this development is the seed of the Pandaemonaeon (Pan-Daemon-Aeon), the melting post-historical pot of possibilities. Here we see the mythical relevance of the model to the present world: it is both a story of the past, and a story of today's world, where the illusion of historical progress collapses into collisions between cultural styles from across the palette of human history.

First Aeon: Oceanic

Key technologies: stone tools, slings for carrying babies, fire, psychedelic plants, language
Social organization: hunter-gatherer, the band
Spirituality: shamanism—animal spirits, ancestors, ecstatic trance ceremonies, communal participation
Time: cyclic, lunar/menstrual rhythms

IT IS PROBABLE that the first calendars were lunar calendars.[3] The rhythm of the moon's waxing and waning is the most basic part of nature from which we can measure time. The rising and setting of the sun is perhaps more basic, giving us the unit of the 'day', but the sun is a constant shining ball of fire. The position on the horizon where it rises and sets alters through the year, but this, like the movements of the stars, is much less obvious than the moon's phases. So the 'moon'—about 28.5 days—became the first unit of time measurement longer than the day (and is still with us as the slightly longer 'month', altered to fit a solar year). Bones with etched marks on them, apparently notches counting lunar cycles, have been found dating back to the Palaeolithic, over 30,000 years ago. These early temporal calculations were probably connected to hunting schedules and other communal rituals.

The other natural rhythms associated with the moon are the ebb and flow of the tides, and the menstrual period in the human female. The first is scientifically associated with the moon through gravitational forces, and may have played a part in early human conceptions of time. The second is the subject of a lot of controversy in terms of its lunar associations. The average menstrual cycle lasts about the same time as a 'moon',

---

3. Interestingly, many mythologies have 'culture heroes', mythic originators of humanity, who are lunar figures.

but not many modern women's periods conform to this. Some say this is due to electric lighting, which abolishes our sensitivity to darkness and the moon's subtle light; but perhaps it is, like the seasons, simply not a totally regular phenomenon.

Still, whatever regularity there is today is certainly affected by modern contraceptives, the stresses of post-industrial culture, and by the needless fuck-ups imposed by a deep history of repressing and despising bodily functions, especially women's bodily functions. Women's periods were probably more regular in prehistoric times, but then again they still had fires to 'disrupt' nature's light and dark. Regularity may have been reinforced by synchronization, where groups of women in close social and emotional contact begin to menstruate in synchrony. There is a lot of debate about the role menstruation may have played in prehistory,[4] but it seems obvious that women's periods would have been at least associated with the earliest measurements of time—or even with the emergence of the concept of time itself. The words 'moon', 'month', and 'menstruation' aren't related by chance.

So the first calendars were not 'abstract'. They were 'organic', anchored to natural rhythms. If it's accepted that lunar calendars were used to co-ordinate social rituals and hunting, we can see that human, experienced time corresponded tangibly with measured time. In other words, if it's time for the full moon feast, you can *see* why—just look up there. Such an intimate association of measured and human time, and a lack of written solidification of the past, leads to present-oriented consciousness. (We should remember the language of the Hopi Indians, which contains no past or future tenses: all 'past' or 'future' events are spoken of in certain variations of the present tense.[5])

'The ancestors' probably formed a focus of shamanic activity in the First Aeon, as they do in contemporary hunter-gatherer (and many other) cultures. In *Life Against Death*, Norman O. Brown (a rampant Freudian with some great ideas) argues that ancestor-based religion denies death. The inability to accept the finality of death, he says, is at the root of our inability to live life to the full. Fear of death undermines our pleasure in life.

Fear of death, of course, comes from an inability to accept birth, separation from

4. *The Wise Wound* by Penelope Shuttle & Peter Redgrove still seems to be the best introduction to this topic. Chris Knight's controversial book *Blood Relations: Menstruation and the Origins of Culture* (see his article 'The Origins of Human Society', http://dreamflesh.com/essays/societyorigins/) is the boldest & most comprehensive attempt to divine the role of menstruation in prehistory, but the author has a great big Marxist axe to grind. He admits it, which is refreshing, but I'd love to hear if anyone had come across less stridently biased research into this area.

5. Arising from the popularization of Benjamin Whorf's often contested work, this theory, as ever, rather simplifies the matter. See http://www.mnsu.edu/emuseum/cultural/language/whorf.html [2007]

the mother, a separation experienced as a kind of dying—the death of unification and the birth of separate individual existence. This may be likened to the birth of humanity, emergent self-consciousness breaking us away from the unified matrix of animal consciousness. Archaic humans, according to Brown, 'conquer death' by living the life of dead ancestors; in many hunter-gatherer tribes today, each person is seen as being infused with the spirit of an ancestor. "This is the pattern of eternal return. Hence archaic society has no real history; and within archaic society there is no individuality. There is no history because there is no individuality; individuality is asserted by breaking with the ancestral archetypes and thus making history."

Whether or not you think societies like this 'deny death' depends on your views on death. Brown sees it as The End. It may well be—but we don't know. Extreme trance states like 'near-death' experiences and potent psychedelic trips sometimes leave people with the conviction that death is merely a transition, and only 'death' to the body and ego. But we won't *really* know until we snuff it. Accepting death—for us, now, at least—seems to be more to do with accepting Uncertainty than accepting The End.

Still, the First Aeon remains the most 'present-conscious' phase of history so far. Christopher Gosden has argued, "There has never been a period in the last 3.5 million years in which natural rhythms were human rhythms, and we have no evidence that Palaeolithic groups were in tune with, or at the mercy of the environment." For him, "Biological rhythms are to human time what sex is to gender; a biological structure that is always worked on culturally." I tend to agree with the last point, and of course he's ultimately in the right about there being no evidence of what was really going on in the Palaeolithic.

But I'm interested in *to what extent* natural rhythms were modified by culture. Hakim Bey, in 'Immediatism', calls for a banishment of mediation in artistic activities, but he is no fool. He admits from the start that "All experience is mediated"—by our bodies and minds at the very least—and calls for a banishment of mediation "at least to the extent that the human condition allows." Palaeolithic lunar-based time structures are certainly a natural rhythm "worked on culturally". But I feel that this cultural modification was minimal, to the extent that the existence of culture allows.

The First Aeon represents low environmental impact and nomadism. Again, there is no such thing as living at one with nature (at least in the narrow worlds of thought and prose that we're in now), but First Aeon lifestyles represent the greatest degree of harmony between human life and the natural environment, to the extent that being human allows.

This Aeon is invoked in experiences of 'oceanic consciousness', a trance that dissolves all inner/ outer boundaries, where time is nothing and the body is all (and all is the body). One perceives one's continuity with the flow of nature, the Tao. Contact with nature spirits and primal energies. Chaos language and glossolalia. Polymorphous sexuality and the group mind.

These statements are not intended to gloss over the harsher aspects of actual life in the First Aeon, or the infinite complexities of the early phases of human culture. They merely attempt to describe our 'key gnosis' of that Aeon, the First Aeon as a present reality in the possibilities of our experience. It does of course have its 'negative' potentials, mainly due to the interference patterns arising between our ego-dominated Aeon and this deeper level of consciousness. I'm not saying that Palaeolithic humans never had a bad time, but that for us First Aeon gnosis can be flipped by the residues of the ego into deep existential terror and fear of death.

For the purposes of this human-centred model, this Aeon overlaps a lot with pre-human atavisms—animal, plant, or even inorganic consciousness. For this reason, I've postulated a 'Zero Aeon' from which all Aeons emanate, infusing all Aeons, containing non-human, organic and inorganic modes of ecstasy: animal group-minds, tree consciousness, rock consciousness, 'The Great Old Ones', possibly also non-terrestrial modes, alien dimensions...

Second Aeon: Seasonal cycles

Key technologies: agriculture, metallurgy, architecture, transport
Social organization: agricultural settlements, the tribe, small cities, divine royalty
Spirituality: paganism—nature gods & goddesses, first 'religions', priesthood elites
Time: cyclic, solar/seasonal rhythms

WITH THE DEVELOPMENT of agriculture, new measurements of time were needed. The cultivation of crops relied on knowledge of the right times to sow and reap, and these times are dictated by the movements of the sun.

Of course, we're actually talking about the movements of the Earth, as it spins in its orbit around the sun. As the planet's axis is tilted slightly, at certain points in its orbit the northern hemisphere tilts away from the sun, and this hemisphere (where agriculture originated) enters winter. The solstices and equinoxes form the basic reference points of the solar year—the longest and shortest days, and the days when the hours of light and dark are equal. Megalithic monuments constructed to pinpoint these solar reference points are common, and as nexuses of social and/or ritual activity, they demonstrate the profound bonds in earlier Aeons between the environment, measured time, and human activities in the world.

The winter solstice seems to have become an important point in the year for agricultural communities. It is the death of the sun, the longest night; but it is also the rebirth of the sun, the point from which days grow longer and longer. The Neolithic passage grave at Newgrange in Ireland is famously connected to the winter solstice. It is constructed so that as the solstice sun rises, a thin shaft of light penetrates the tomb through a narrow slit, illuminating the back wall of the burial chamber for about seventeen minutes. Such an elaborately constructed monument shows how important the cycles of the sun were to the agricultural Neolithic.

Time is connected to sex, and to death. The reborn sun's shaft of light is seen by some to represent a big cock penetrating the darkness of the tomb/womb, bestowing life on the concealed dead. The connection between time and death has been most succinctly expressed by William Burroughs: "Death needs time for what it kills to grow in." (*Dead City Radio*) It is also expressed mythically in the Indian black goddess Kali, "the symbol of the active cosmic power of eternal time ... she signifies annihilation: through death or destruction creation, the seed of life, emerges." (Mookerjee & Khanna, *The Tantric Way*) So we might tantrically elaborate on Burroughs by saying: "Time needs death for what it grows to die in."

When discussing the sun 'reanimating the dead' in Newgrange, we may well be moving into metaphorical realms, where we may speak of death and birth in terms of decaying and emerging ideas, identities, beliefs and forms within the world of the living. No one with all their marbles intact believes in the literal, bodily resurrection of the dead; but metaphorical resurrection of the dead, whether in terms of ancestor spirits or solar-agricultural beliefs in cyclicity, is obviously a powerful focus in early Aeons for time-transcending structures of belief.

'Metaphorical' here does not mean 'unreal' or 'abstract'. It refers to aspects of life that evade our definition of 'literal'. We, looking back, can only describe the death and birth of the sun, or the resurrection of the dead, as metaphorical, lacking a better word. But imagine a Neolithic priestess waiting with supremely focused awe and expectation for the winter solstice sunlight inside Newgrange... drums pounding, consciousness altering, senses honed and opened... That dazzling shaft of light would have induced a psychosomatic fusion of mythical perceptions and ecstatic feelings of such potency that if you could have gone up to her afterwards and told her what had just happened was 'unreal' and 'abstract', she would have rightly smacked you in the face for being impertinent.

An important point to note here, as we're using Newgrange as a 'testing ground' for ideas, is that, due to the size of the chamber, only a small group of people could have witnessed this great event at the solstice. The monument was probably built by hundreds of people. Evidently we've got major social division going on here, with some kind of priest-class attending to important rituals. Such social division probably emerged very early on in human culture—look at Ice Age cave paintings in France, in small recesses which were only accessible through narrow and convoluted passages.

But as far as temporal reference-points go, people of the First Aeon can see their moon wax and wane whoever and wherever they were. In the Second Aeon, larger social groups lead to greater social stratification. Monuments like Newgrange, which is not unique, demonstrate how human creativity and engineering became necessary to focus the less tangible solar reference-points. And the focal points were only accessible to a chosen few. The social divisions were not necessarily as closely linked with oppression and control as our experience of social divisions has conditioned us to expect, but they were there.

Second Aeon time is still cyclic, but it seems that broader units of measured time lead to a greater gulf between measured and human time. 'Present-consciousness' seems to be squashed a bit and made more diffuse by awareness of longer time spans.

The Second Aeon sees the development of the first major calendars. The Mayan calendar is a fine example of a large-scale pagan calendar, and one whose existence nicely demonstrates the non-linear, non-progressive nature of 'global time'. Firstly, this Second Aeon culture was just emerging in Mesoamerica when European cultures were 'progressing' well into their Third Aeon. Secondly, the fact that the 'Long Count' calendar's 5,125 years were theoretically preceded and succeeded by other equally extensive cyclical periods means that the Mayans (or at least the Mayan priesthood) were capable of envisioning vast spans of time.

Compare this with the Christian church's record. In the seventeenth century, the Archbishop of Armargh, James Usher, famously worked out that Earth was created in 4,004 BCE—using the genealogical evidence from that venerable work of historical accuracy, the Bible. This chronology only came into question through pioneering geological work in the late eighteenth century.

From this we can see several things. Our culture is *not* some sort of pinnacle of knowledge. Also, greater spans of measured time (like the Mayan calendar) do not necessarily imply more and more abstraction from the present and from ecstasy—the Mayans were well versed in ecstatic experience. Nor do greater spans of measured time imply a greater level of technological development (or vice versa), as a linear view of the history of time might imply—the Mayans were a technologically stone age culture.

The Second Aeon represents a more settled lifestyle, and a deeper level of imposition on the environment, though this activity is still felt to be interactive. The Earth is still felt to be a living being, but it is worked upon, worked with, cultivated. Simple First Aeonic reverence for natural landscape features is embellished with physically constructed landscape features like megalithic temples and tombs. The first large towns and cities emerge, sowing the seeds of withdrawal from the natural environment. The first signs of written languages appear.

It is interesting to note here the common view that preliterate cultures—'traditional' peoples—are not given to development and 'progress'. This is a prejudice. Deep immersion in cyclic time does not preclude cultural and spiritual evolution and transformation. Preliteracy merely limits significant material, *technological* progress. As soon as writing was invented, and material technologies like metal-working and more efficient methods of transport were developed, it seems that human society entered a faster, more frenetic stream of evolution. One in which technological evolution far outruns cultural and spiritual evolution.

The Second Aeon is invoked in experiences of interactive trance, where individual identity is maintained to an extent, but relationship to the environment is harmonious and involved. Personal ecstasy that can be transmitted and received—shared. Awareness that the experience has begun and will end is sometimes present, but the anxiety this knowledge can cause can be worked through and transformed into creative energy. Contact with godforms which have emerged from long-term large-scale human belief, expressing personal and social drives and qualities. Poetry and song. Sex in terms of defined but playful and inter-changeable roles. Ego interference can cause rather intense (though potentially more creative) versions of the Third Aeon trance—see later.

Third Aeon: History

Key technologies: writing, large-scale transport & architecture

Social organization: the family, city-states, empires, divine royalty

Spirituality: monotheism ('one god')—ecstatic religion driven underground, competing religions violently suppressed, paganism appropriated & abstracted

Time: linear, eschatological ('the end of the world'), natural rhythms desacralized, sacred time seen as existing far in the past or future

BETWEEN THE SECOND AND THIRD AEONS we have, from the magical point of view, a cataclysmic transformation: the development of monotheism. Along with this dictatorial cosmology came the brutal suppression of ecstatic traditions, which were rightly seen to undermine the spiritual authority of the priesthoods—and thus their political power. First-hand spirituality became a touchy subject in an era where second-hand spirituality was one of the major political tools of suppression and control.[6]

Of course, polytheistic paganism and ecstatic first-hand spirituality did not vanish. The actual conflicts and interactions of history are far more complex than that. Pagan elements are in fact the source of many major elements in the monotheistic religions. Jesus is certainly a mutation of pagan vegetation or solar gods, being born *oh!* so close to the midwinter solstice when the sun is reborn, and coming back to life in spring-time after his literalized shamanic 'death'. Pagan elements were subsumed into the borderlines and nether regions of monotheism, often retaining great power among rural 'heathens'—as in the veneration of the Blessed Virgin Mary among people whose ancestors worshipped the nature-goddesses, and among native Mexicans, who happily carried on munching mushrooms when they learnt that their invading Catholic rulers also ate 'god's flesh' in their ceremonies. Monotheistic traditions are not without their just-tolerated ecstasies, like Islam's Sufi orders and the enraptured mystics dotted about Christianity's heritage. Genuine pagan ecstasies, however, became 'occult', hidden. They went underground.

As an expression of a certain historical tendency, the Third Aeon is characterized by a narrow, arrogant, destructive and decidedly anti-nature stance towards the world: an unchecked preponderance of the ego and a fear of bodily and supra-bodily trances. The swelling of the ego is expressed in the growth in importance of the city as a focus for human life, an island of culture with invisible, atrophying links to the natural environment.

When Christians first distinguished themselves from pagans, the word 'pagan' meant 'country-dweller'. For the first centres of Christianity in the Roman Empire were the

6. The Second-to-Third Aeon transition is the 'classic' fuck-up in history from the point of view of most pagans. But most pagans are barely politicized, and don't mind the social divisions of the Second Aeon (or this one for that matter). We should also consider the view that the inauguration of the Second Aeon, the development of agriculture, was the 'Fall' in human history. "Agriculture is the only radical new technology that ever appeared in the world; what it amounts to is a cutting into the earth. If you read any anthropology about Native Americans, you will find that when the white Europeans arrived and tried to force the tribes into agriculture, the tribal people always say the same thing: 'What, you want us to rape our Mother, the Earth? This is perverse. How could you ask human beings to do this?' Agriculture immediately appears as a bad deal to these tribes. There is no doubt that this technology leads inevitably and fairly quickly to social hierarchies, separation, class structure, property, and religion as we understand it—a priest class that tells everybody else what to do and how to think. It leads, in other words, to authoritarianism and, ultimately, to the state itself." (Peter Lamborn Wilson, 'Cybernetics & Entheogenics: From Cyberspace to Neurospace')

great cities—Antioch, Corinth, Alexandria, and Rome itself.

Alan Watts, *Nature, Man & Woman*

Such concentration of populations in settlements was probably necessary to focus resource distribution, though, and short of population control (not easy when God tells you to "be fruitful and multiply") this was the only way of avoiding severe stresses on habitated landscapes.

Third Aeon time becomes linear. The cycle of the seasons is, of course, still present; but as communal ecstasies wither, the succession of years becomes an endless succession, never looping back on itself or dipping into atemporal phases of ritual renewal. Time is desacralized, made profane.

Contemporary shamanic hunter-gatherers have their Edenic myths of lost archaic paradises, and their eschatological future catastrophe myths. But the paradisiacal/catastrophic zones of sacred time are related to 'profane' present time through communal rituals and the activities of shamans. First and Second Aeon cultures maintain a connection to non-ordinary time; and anyhow, their very conception of 'profane' time and space is usually radically different from that of Third Aeon consciousness.

In 'Making Time', Bob Trubshaw quotes a description of a Navaho native American craftswoman who, "instead of standing on a straight ribbon of time leading from the past to some future point, stands in the middle of a vortex of forces exerted in concentric circles upon her by her immediate family, her extended family, the clan, the tribe, and the whole living ecological system within which she lives and functions. ... Time surrounds her, as do the dwelling place, her family, her clan, her tribe, her habitat, her dances, her rituals." Similarly, Trubshaw discusses nomadic Mongolian tribes, for whom the 'centre of the world', the *axis mundi*, is located wherever they set up camp, represented by the central pole of the tent or the smoke rising up from the central hearth. Through this mobile *axis mundi* they are always connected to the deified sky, "the power above all powers and the only deity regarded as eternal." And their temporal connections to the eternal sky eventually spiral round as they revisit camp-sites each year.

Eschatologies and sacred/profane divisions of time are not exclusive to the Third Aeon. What is significant about this phase is the flattening of time-concepts into a cumulative, progressive experience of time, with a reduction of experienced atemporality and renewal in this world. Certain lingering pagan festivities allowed a measure of sacred time into people's lives, but essentially atemporality and renewal are postponed; not now, later. Be patient. The Kingdom of God, the New Jerusalem will come—soon, sometime... (never). The carrot-on-a-stick metaphor is apt, considering the Third Aeon's progressive alienation from the land and agricultural rhythms.

Central to linear time conceptions is fundamentalist soul/body dualism. "The divorce between soul and body takes the life out of the body, reducing the organism to a mechanism." (Norman Brown, *Love's Body*) Similarly, divorcing sacred time from human, experienced time, and locating it in some extra-terrestrial cloud-cuckoo-land far in the future, reduces this world to a profane burden. History is never renewed, it just marches on, dragging more and more of itself behind it and getting clogged up with the stale residue of the past.

The oppression of women and the repression of femininity is a key feature of the Third Aeon. The menstrual/lunar rhythms of the First Aeon and the close relationship to the fruitful body of the Earth of the Second Aeon are left behind. One God is always male, and women are viewed with suspicion and contempt as allies of the Devil. Again, oppression of women and repression of femininity are not the sole property of the Third Aeon, but it is here that they reach massively destructive levels.

This Aeon is invoked in non-participatory trances—egoistic inflation which can lose its balance and slip into aggression, arrogance and intolerance, but may be personally empowering. The world is faced in an attitude of confrontation—sometimes necessary in our disjointed and often hostile society, though this trance has a tendency to feed on itself until it breaks down, a painful experience. Linear time conceptions often imbue this trance with a sense of frustration and urgency, the feeling that something needs to happen... it's not happening now, but it needs to happen as soon as possible. Contact with the non-ecstatic God, the ego-deity of blinkered vision and self-importance. Dictatorial language and 'objective', unambiguous prose. Exploitative sexuality, sometimes enjoyed but often tinged with a sense of loss or emptiness (usually after the ego's selfish pleasures are punctured by orgasm). Of course, we're now at the stage where 'ego interference' is not an issue!

Fourth Aeon: Imperial Science

Although time and space may seem to us to form a neutral, objective framework, this framework was constructed with empires in mind...

Christopher Gosden, *Social Being and Time*

Key technologies: the telescope, the microscope, electricity, telecommunications, guns, bombs

Social organization: the nuclear family, industrial urbanism, nationalism

Spirituality: atheistic scientism—total loss of ecstatic traditions, empty religious formalities performed through habit, spirituality debunked, first attempts at reviving paganism

Time: linear, unchanging & theoretically infinite, possible cosmological end in entropic heat death of the universe, no sacred time, faith in material utopias grows & dies quickly & repeatedly

THIS AEON IS THE EMPTY SHELL of the Third—not much fun, eh?

It is the first reliably 'dateable' Aeon; it seems to have fully emerged in Europe during the last few hundred years. It also appears to be much more complex than previous Aeons—but probably just because it is closer to us, and has left more self-documentation.

Science is the major factor. The objective study of the world split further and further away from religious traditions, and came to provide the dominant myth-structures—dangerous ones at that, since the package they came in had "THIS IS NOT A MYTH" stamped on it. The literalism of the Third Aeon reaches full bloom here.

The Bible, for example, is a potent cocktail of myth and history that came to be seen as just literal history by its editors, the Christian Church. De-mythologizing hardened this text into a tool, or a weapon, used to control the populace—"God says that's bad!"—and to bolster self-importance to a level where you're incapable of tolerating other views, other myths—"Ours is the One True Religion. You heathens have mere cults, your myths are fanciful, nay, demonic falsehoods." Fourth Aeon scientism (science as religion) shifted its faith from the Word of God to the evidence of the senses—at least the five sanctioned by scientism itself, and even those only under sober and rigorous constraints. The desacralization of the world proceeded, and all magical perceptions—even that silly magic of believing in the total authority of one book—were banished through belief in the literal primacy of material reality.

Materialism is deceptive, though. It is a curious belief, in that it manages to forget its foundations in the very system it refuses to confront—the mind. Descartes' philosophy is often seen as one of the pillars of materialism, yet he managed to divorce mind and body, "reducing the organism to a mechanism", through intellectual analysis. The world had to be *conceptualized* as a machine before it could be taken apart and analysed *as if it were* a machine that obeyed fixed, eternal, physical laws.

A more magical, less philosophical, interpretation of this development is that human culture lost touch with ecstatic states of consciousness, and thus with perception of the multi-levelled nature of reality and the felt mystery at the heart of existence. Fear of altered states becomes stronger and stronger the less they are experienced, resulting in the sober illusions of 'ordinary consciousness' and 'objectivity'.

Alan Watts once pointed out the paradox of materialism with elegant simplicity: "It is strictly incorrect to think of progressive cultures as materialistic, if the materialist is one who loves concrete materials. No modern city looks as if it were made by people who love material." (*Nature, Man & Woman*) Damn right! Modern cities were made by people who believed that only solid, literal, materials exist, and were thus seldom touched by the love for the world—this world, the very one they place their faith in—that is fuelled by the ecstasies that they banished with their philosophy. Humans really make things complicated for themselves...

Fourth Aeon time is a totally desacralized progression from Third Aeon time. It's as linear as fuck, and totally removed from the structures that govern it—our body chemistry, our social rituals, etc. Isaac Newton saw measured time as "Absolute, true, and mathematical time, of itself, and from its own nature, [which] flows equally without relation to anything external."[7]

The Biblical creation myth is eventually replaced by the myths of the Big Bang and evolution. The Apocalypse of St John is replaced by the eventual decline of galactic systems, entropy increasing until everything just fizzles out—with nothing to follow. Without Zen, this is not a good prospect. Shorter-term utopian visions, fed by the leftovers of New Jerusalem, arose from the truly astounding technological advancements made in this Aeon.

The social and political structuring of time in this Aeon is especially interesting. It is here that our present system of 'global time' was constructed. The expansion of capitalist empires across the world led to the need for a synchronization of measured time:

> *In the 1870s there were over 200 local times between the east and west coasts of the USA, which made the running of a unified national rail system very difficult. In 1883 this confusion was resolved through the imposition of a series of time zones across the nation. In the following year time and space were linked in a global system when it was agreed that Greenwich should become the zero meridian and world time should be measured from there.*

Christopher Gosden, Social Being and Time

In 1912 at the International Conference on Time in Paris, it was agreed that telegraphs would be used to beam time signals around the globe to keep the capitalist

7. Quoted in Gosden, p. 2.

machinery ticking in an orderly fashion. Time is money, don'tcha know?

This rigorous standardization of measured time goes hand-in-hand with the total disappearance of sacred time:

> *The ancient concepts of jubilee and saturnalia originate in an intuition that certain events lie outside the scope of "profane time," the measuring-rod of the State and of History. These holidays literally occupied gaps in the calendar—intercalary intervals. By the Middle Ages, nearly a third of the year was given over to holidays. Perhaps the riots against the calendar reform had less to do with the "eleven lost days" than with a sense that imperial science was conspiring to close up these gaps in the calendar where the people's freedoms had accumulated—a coup d'etat, a mapping of the year, a seizure of time itself, turning the organic cosmos into a clockwork universe. The death of the festival.*

Hakim Bey, The Temporary Autonomous Zone

A probably unforeseen consequence of imperialist expansion was the feedback the Fourth Aeon began to get from the First and Second Aeon cultures it bumped into (and didn't wipe out). Such contact had begun during the Third Aeon, but it was not until large-scale invasion of older cultures began, with economic motives, that the feedback became significant. The academic discipline of anthropology is rooted in the attempts of Western nations to gather information about 'the natives'—all the better to control them. But this information began to work its way into the cracks of the already tottering and shaky edifice of the Fourth Aeon, confirming doubts and inspiring resistance. Marx and Engels' ideas were greatly influenced by information coming into Europe about hunter-gatherer societies. Ethnology and anthropology began to feed into the revival of interest in paganism and magic at the turn of the century, too, along with the 'Wisdom of the East'. Imperial feedback is complex—it can feed imperialism itself, racism in overt and subtle forms, misappropriation of alien cultures, and so on. It can also feed those living in the source of the Empire who are oppressed by it themselves, and are looking for a way out from a sick society.

We don't need to do much to invoke the Fourth Aeon—it still lies close. Its primary trance is that of the mundane—formal social trances, industrial work trances, empty pious church-going trances, all the trances of ingrained habit and dull duty. The world is not so much 'faced' as endured; it often seems pointless and absurd. A feeling that you're not 'at home', wherever you are. This trance can rarely be maintained for long without 'worrying' glitches arising, basic life energies revolting against such an encrusted surface of restraint. These glitches can build up into destructive outbreaks of frustrated Third Aeon self-assertion and aggression, or mild breakdowns; though sometimes one can just slide in the other direction and enter a pleasant realm of acceptance more reminiscent of the Second Aeon. But this acceptance, of course, is often fuel for the continuance of the mundanity trance. There is often an odd pseudo-transcendence of the ego at work here, as anyone who's done long shifts in a factory can testify. Fourth Aeon time goes on and on and on and on and on.... and on. Contact with nothing in particular. Language flattened into platitudes and monosyllables. Dutiful sex that can only be called sex because of what's going on physically. Even the ego gets pissed off with this trance, and can rabbit on incessantly to keep itself busy and make you confused.

Fifth Aeon: Chaos Rising

May you live in interesting times.   Apocryphal Chinese curse

Key technologies: LSD, television, the computer, spacecraft, nuclear fission, the amplifier & the loudspeaker

Social organization: multinational corporations, social control as a self-supporting illusion, social fragmentation, the extended 'found' family

Spirituality: chaotic—existential panic & alienated numbness, last-ditch attempts at monotheistic fundamentalism (with some ecstatic elements), re-emergence & fabrication of past traditions, adoption of foreign traditions, post-scientific models, new traditions & mythologies (UFOs), open-ended ecstatic dance ceremonies, chemical gnosis

Time: chaotic, with a tight facade of linearity kept as habitual hang-over from the past, eschatologies from fear of ecological disaster, awareness of the 'history of time'

ONE COULD TRACE ELEMENTS of this Aeon right back through history—because it is here that Aeonic feedback intensifies at an alarming rate—but for our vague chronological purposes, it seems to have been precipitated by the Second World War and its fallout.

Fallout indeed. The bombs dropped on Nagasaki and Hiroshima in 1945 added to the doubts about technological progress that had resulted from the First World War. And these monumental events, along with the awareness of an approaching new millennium in the Gregorian calendar, and awareness of the nastier side-effects of in-dustrialism on the biosphere, increased eschatological feelings to a level not seen since medieval times. This is where the weight of history accumulated by linear, 'progressive' time becomes unbearable, threatening to drag us screaming back down the ladder we feel we've climbed—unless we cast it off. Or see that we're not climbing a ladder, we're running around in a maze of our own making.

Aleister Crowley's Aeonic model held that we have progressed through the Aeon of Isis (the Mother) during pagan times, and through the Aeon of Osiris (the Father) during monotheistic times. And now we've entered the Aeon of Horus (the Child), which he believed he had initiated in 1904 by 'receiving' *The Book of the Law* from his Guardian Angel Aiwass.[8] Crowley's magical and philosophical achievements can be seen as being prophetic of our Fifth Aeon, in the way he consciously synthesized systems from different cultures and traditions; but he lived, like Nietzsche, ahead of his time, and paid dearly for his anachronism (as well as for his egotism). The fifties' Beat Movement caught the flow of culture just about right, and it's hard to work out if they initiated, or were just there at the birth of the Fifth Aeon's vanguard, the 'youth revolution'—the empowerment of those who had yet to fully inherit the corrupt power of the Fourth Aeon.

Now that our model has caught up with 'present time', things get intensely complicated—not that they aren't in earlier Aeons, it's just that we have less distance from our own Aeon, and generalizations become harder to casually dish out. But what are the basic characteristics of the past fifty years or so?

In terms of grand political structures, Burroughs saw it coming early:

> We have a new type of rule now. Not one-man rule, or rule of aristocracy or plutoc-racy, but of small groups elevated to positions of absolute power by random pressures, and subject to political and economic factors that leave little room for decisions. ... The rulers of this most insecure of all worlds are rulers by accident, inept, frightened pilots at the controls of a vast machine they cannot understand, calling in experts to tell them which buttons to push.
>
> *Interzone*

The empires created by the Fourth Aeon have grown out of the control of their creators. The social divisions that serve the interests of power elites and the wealthy have become self-perpetuating, fuelled and reinforced by loops of image-based control-

8. As Monica Sjöö says in her article 'Sinister New Age Channellings', 'channelled' texts are often good excuses for passing off responsibility for views and opinions onto intangible authors. Crowley did this to an extent, excusing some of the more dubious sections of the book in this way, but for the most part he took the responsibility implied in the text unto himself with gusto. In the end, he thought he was the initiator of the New Aeon, not Aiwass. Evidently he had not totally shrugged off the egoistic Third Aeon.

mantras coursing through the mass media. Democracy has quickly become a total illusion. Power seems to have shifted from governments, who become more and more like each other to appeal to everyone's insecurities, to unaccountable multinational corporations and media conglomerates.

And while I'm well aware that multinational CEOs and media giants like Rupert Murdoch never suffer in anything like the way that their victims (indigenous peoples, the impoverished, the marginalized) do, I can't help wondering if these people are actually in control of things. "Control is controlled by its need to control." And ruthless capitalists are controlled by their need to make money. The paradox of power has been there since the beginning. Pagan kings were regularly killed sacrificially, because their symbolic position, representing the fertility of the land and the vigour of the kingdom, was too important for them to grow old, fat and lazy. Today's Kings of Capital grow old and fat… but rarely lazy. Just more and more insecure, and very, very rich. To what end? Hedonistic debauchery and idle languishing in the pleasures of the world? No, they're too concerned with fucking people over and making unmonitored deals to gain more income, more 'control', more 'power'. They gain the world—which is nothing if you don't enjoy it—and lose their souls in piles of money.

Conspiracy theories are popular now for good and bad reasons. Good: people are more and more suspicious of what is hidden from them by their governments. Bad: people desperately want to believe that large-scale 'control' still exists, be it the enigmatic Illuminati, Rupert Murdoch, friendly aliens, or hostile aliens. Is this all nostalgia for God? Embedded in a social structure that seems to be beyond their personal control, people seem to be hoping that someone is in control, so they can either place their faith in them or rebel against them. In many instances, the heart of control has actually been diffused, and infests the fabric of our everyday lives. Sometimes it abstracts itself to a point where it can rightly be seen as illusion, to be broken through spontaneous acts of non-participation in the illusion, refusal to give it substance.

This doesn't stop police sticking telescopic truncheons in your face if you test the illusion a little too much, or a little too blatantly. It is here that control can be tested, to see just how much of it is illusory. Some acts, like gathering to protest against governmental policy, are met with force and violence. This is, from a certain point of view, encouraging. As Burroughs has pointed out, a fully functioning police state doesn't need to use physical violence—its citizens conform quietly without question. The increase in police powers in recent years is worrying, like the rise in fundamentalist Christianity. But, as with Christianity, it is really evidence of crumbling authority, a last-ditch show of force, like someone giving their all too hang on to the edge of a precipice just before they know they are going to fall.

Much of this Aeon's characteristics are merely attempts to mask the collapse of the last couple of Aeons. Most have admitted to this collapse, at least in their more private moments. Many run around whining about it publicly. Some have welcomed it, and revel in it. Some have welcomed it, and are busy getting on with the business of creating something new. Few escape the falling ruins of religious and scientific monoliths, though, and this Aeon is not so much to do with a 'clean break' into fresh new pastures, but with turbulent attempts to come to terms with the realities of uncertainty and personal responsibility that are revealed as our institutional guardians crumble to the ground. Those who survive will be those who find joy in these attempts, and mutate.

Measured time marches on, tightened by digital precision and further economic globalization. Human, experienced time, emerging as it does from social rituals and communal experiences of work and play, becomes more chaotic and fragmented. Shifting patterns of work, the fragmentation of communities and cultures, the increased use of psychotropic chemicals, deeper awareness of the relativity of time-experience itself... all contribute to the breakdown of consensus human time. The tension between the tightening of measured time and the fragmentation of human time manifests in concerns about the approaching millennium, which has been seized upon by state and religion alike as a focus for 'unification', 'renewal', and other euphemisms for the regeneration of their waning powers.

This Aeon is not invoked, it is present. Like the clash between measured and human time, the tension between the hyper-efficiency of the media-generated 'conformity trance', and the vast range of possible non-conformist trances open to us now, has lead to widespread instability and mental illness. The ego is fed to bursting point with images and word-viruses and 'double-binds', like adverts that recycle postmodernism and use anti-commercialism as a selling point. Identity is supported by work and consumption, and is thus as unstable and unreal as the 'spectacular' late capitalist economy itself. On the other hand, Aeonic feedback has reached a crescendo, and there are probably more people today with access to the liberatory power of First and Second Aeon trances than there have ever been on the planet at once. Of course, vast amounts of this feedback is diverted straight into the consumerist identity-pool.

Self-identity here is fragmented—varieties of schizophrenia and/or immense flexibility. Contact with anything and everything, from bar-coded deities of the New Age to pissed-off nature spirits, from Grey Aliens (primal daimons taking the piss out of scientism[9]) to

---

9. See *Daimonic Reality* by Patrick Harpur.

merry elves celebrating the downfall of monotheism. Chaotic language: recycled media-bites, pseudo-religious corporate jargon, (p)unrestrained word-play, cut-ups and samples. Chaotic sexuality: from orgone shut-down and numbness to conscious sado-masochism (Fourth and Third Aeon sexual impulses harnessed to invoke the Second and First Aeons); from transexualism to non-bodily fetishism (e.g. cars); from faceless promiscuity to group marriages.

The Pandaemonaeon

NOT NECESSARILY THE 'NEXT' AEON; it is already here. From a certain point of view, it always has been here, only now erupting with more frequency and intensity. It is not an amoral free-for-all, at least not in the sense understood by the corrupt and repressive moralism of, say, Christianity. It is an immediate awareness of the pin-point vortex of freedom within us all, into which all habit and illusion may be allowed to fall, and from which emanates an enormous responsibility. That is, response-ability: not day-to-day acknowledgement of our involuntary duties, but moment-to-moment acknowledgement of our connection to the world.

The Pandaemonaeon is a rejection of futurism too, a refusal to redeem the present through hope in the future.

The present often seems dismal, hopeless, a prison. Two possibilities. Perhaps the prison is not your situation, but your perception of it, a perception fed by the opinions of others who have different ideals and desires. Try to banish outside influences for a while and divine your own desires.

Or perhaps it is a prison. In which case, don't wait for parole, start digging! Life is not a waiting room…

Bibliography

Bey, Hakim, *The Temporary Autonomous Zone* (Autonomedia, 1991)

— 'Immediatism', on *T.A.Z.* (Axiom Records, 1994)

— 'Millennium'

Brown, Norman O., *Life Against Death: The Psychoanalytical Meaning of History* (Wesleyan University, 1959)

— *Love's Body* (Vintage, 1966)

Burroughs, William S., *The Ticket That Exploded* (Corgi, 1971)

— *Interzone* (Picador, 1990)

— *Dead City Radio* (Island Records, 1990)

Caruana, Wally, *Aboriginal Art* (Thames & Hudson, 1993)

Chatwin, Bruce, *The Songlines* (Picador, 1987)

Gosden, Christopher, *Social Being and Time* (Blackwell, 1994)

Gyrus (ed.), *Towards 2012* part III: 'Culture & Language' (The Unlimited Dream Company, 1997)

— *The Devil & the Goddess* (Norlonto, 2000)

Hine, Phil, *Prime Chaos* (Chaos International, 1993)

Lee, Dave, *Chaotopia! Magick and Ecstasy in the PandaemonAeon* (Attractor, 1997)

Mookerjee, Ajit & Khanna, Madhu, *The Tantric Way* (Thames & Hudson, 1977)

Taylor, Timothy, *The Prehistory of Sex* (Fourth Estate, 1996)

Trubshaw, Bob, 'Exploring Past and Place' in *At The Edge* no. 1, March 1996 (http://www.indigogroup.co.uk/edge/explore.htm)

— 'Making Time' in *At The Edge* no. 7, September 1997 (http://www.indigogroup.co.uk/edge/makingt.htm)

Weir, Anthony, 'Time & Place: The TV of our minds' in *At The Edge* no. 1, March 1996 (http://www.indigogroup.co.uk/edge/Timeplac.htm)

Wilson, Peter Lamborn, 'Cybernetics & Entheogenics: From Cyberspace to Neurospace' (http://www.t0.or.at/hakimbey/neurospc.htm)

THE ORIGINS
OF MUSIC,
LANGUAGE,
MIND AND BODY

THE SINGING
NEANDERTHALS

Steven Mithen

'Extraordinary . . . a new and controversial theory
of the origins of language and music'
Sunday Telegraph

THE SINGING NEANDERTHALS

THE ORIGINS OF MUSIC, LANGUAGE, MIND AND BODY

by Steven Mithen

This review was first published on dreamflesh.com in 2006.

G IVEN THE RAPID RATE at which our images of human prehistory are changing, thanks to the speed of archaeological progress, Steven Mithen's 1996 book *The Prehistory of the Mind* is quite old news. I read it for the first time recently while camping in Galicia, and was both thrilled and frustrated by it. Thrilled because it painted perhaps the most coherent and sensitive picture of the evolution of human consciousness I've encountered; but frustrated by its frankly bizarre neglect of the possibilities raised by what we call "altered states", altered by plants or otherwise.

The Singing Neanderthals hits a similar balance, this time honing in on the role of language and music in our journey from the world of apes, through various hominid branches, to our present identity as *Homo sapiens*. Mithen rallies the very latest research in archaeology (much of his evidence having arisen just a year or two before publication), plus insights from a broad survey of relevant disciplines, taking in developmental psychology, neuropathology, ethological studies of primate behaviour, and naturally a liberal dash of musicology and linguistics. His ability to sift through vast amounts of scientific data, to weigh findings in different arenas against each other, and synthesize conclusions using both common sense and methodical rigour, is hugely impressive. As is, equally importantly, his knack for expressing this process vividly, never coming across as condescending when trying to make something clear, and never getting carried away with his profession's jargon.

It's disappointing, then, to find the same odd neglect of altered states. Let me be clear; despite this topic being one of my personal hobby horses, I think this is an objectively sound criticism, not just a strained cry of, "Talk about *my* things!" The very nature of Mithen's theories, in both books, almost begs for altered states to be factored in. His conclusions are perhaps the best support I've come across for the theory that altered states—especially, of course, plant hallucinogens—may have played a crucial role in the evolution of consciousness. Many will understandably remark that I'm asking too much of a professional archaeologist—they never talk about the weird shit, do they? Well, they do these days.[1] This new wave of consideration for hallucinations and trances naturally has its detractors, who range from well-meaning scientists making valid critical observations to obsessively antagonistic fuddy-duddies with frightful, misshapen axes to grind. What is bizarre is that Mithen is neither. He doesn't even address the subject to dismiss it. Such avoidance can only be wilful, and the charitable guess is that he wants to have the meat of his theories digested by his colleagues and wider public without the unfortunate whiff of hysteria that often surrounds discussion of psychedelics. Fair enough; but while such political considerations are often an unavoidable part of science, they are nevertheless distasteful and distorting.

THE PREHISTORY OF THE MIND proposed that the higher apes, and then hominids, evolved a few "hard-wired" types of intelligence, often referred to as "modules" or "domains". Mithen takes those that came to be genetically encoded into hominid brains to be:

Social intelligence, helping to navigate the increasingly complex nature of hominid interactions
Technical intelligence, forming the basis of our leaps forward from the basic tool-use

1. My hypertext links this phrase to my review of David Lewis-Williams' *The Mind in the Cave*, a fine summary of the argument for the role of trance in prehistoric cave art (http://dreamflesh.com/reviews/mindcave/).

found in other animals

Natural history intelligence, basically framing our knowledge and thinking about the rest of the natural world around us

The core of his theory in that book was that hominids from the early *Australopithecines* through to the Neanderthal dead-end evolved each of these types of intelligence, but it was only *Homo sapiens* who made the breakthrough. That is, breaking through the barriers that until then seemed to have isolated these mental domains from each other. Mithen held that developments in the linguistic faculties of humans led to the ability to *see one domain in terms of another*, i.e. to think metaphorically. This neatly explains why,

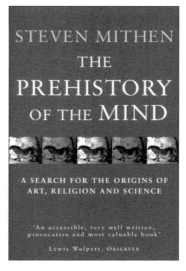

for instance, we find quite advanced tool use among early hominids (almost no modern humans can replicate the flint-knapping skills of the Neanderthals), but at best scant, debatable evidence of symbolic thinking or art. Mithen holds that what we recognize as art, religion, or science arise from a "cognitive fluidity" that lets us bring one form of intelligence to bear on another. Thus, when technical intelligence is applied to social thinking, we get the creation of artefacts, like jewellery and clothing, that communicate social signals. Similarly, when social and natural history intelligence are fused, we can personify nature, think of social structures in terms of animal relationships (totemism), and imagine the human-animal hybrids that are ubiquitous in mythology and prehistoric art.

(Seeing one thing in terms of another, metaphorical thinking, cognitive fluidity, novel combinations and juxtapositions… Are any mushroom-shaped bells ringing for you?)

Given that language is seen as one of main engines of change in this process, *The Singing Neanderthals* is probably a necessary follow-up. This is made plain during its conclusion, where the crucial shift in vocal expression engendered by *Homo sapiens* is seen in the development of *compositional* language, i.e. language made up of discreet words that can be juggled around according to syntactical rules to compose an infinity of expressions. It's this ability to mix and recombine elements that ties the ideas here back to the theory of consciousness so convincingly set out in *Prehistory of the Mind*.

But what about before compositional language? This forms the bulk of Mithen's theorizing here. Noting the differences and similarities between music and language (explained via fascinating excursions into case histories of people with various forms of brain damage), he eventually concludes that the debate about which came first is a chicken-and-egg dead end resulting from framing the debate wrongly. He believes *both* came first, that music and language have a common ancestor: a melodic form of proto-language used by hominids right up until we started mashing it all up.

Popular science writing hinges, funnily enough, on metaphorical thinking, on the author's ability to find the most striking balance in his central metaphor between accurately representing the theory and capturing the reader's imagination. In *Prehistory of the Mind* he used the image of the mind as a cathedral, with each "domain" as a chapel within it; it served admirably. (It also tickled me when I read the conclusion, in which he sees it as apt that he finished the book in Santiago de Compostela, famed for its cathedral—I was camping very close to the city at the time.) Here, the metaphor doesn't work so well. To be precise, there's no metaphor, just an acronym. And not a great acronym at that: "Hmmmmm". It stands for what he sees this proto-language as being: Holistic, manipulative, multi-modal, musical and mimetic. It's cute in a way, but it really doesn't flow well on the page; even less so, I suspect, in speech.

In any case, *holism* means that he sees pre-human speech as having been a collection of expressive utterances, certainly a good few syllables at a time, but crucially not made up of re-arrangeable words. And they would be mostly *manipulative*, translating into compositional language as things like "Go over there" or "Share that meat with her". *Multi-modal* emphasizes that body language, gestures and movement would have played a much more central role in "Hmmmmm" communication. The *musical* element is, similarly, still present in our language in how we intone speech and give it rhythm (something that linguistics, as Mithen portrays it, has persistently neglected, much to its detriment); but again, "Hmmmmm" sees this playing a much greater role. Finally, *mimesis* can be seen in the image of hominid hunters trying to communicate information to each other about their quarry by expressing its qualities and attributes.

THE REASONING AND EVIDENCE on all these points is lucid, interesting and convincing. Notable is part of the background against which Mithen develops this thesis: the idea that "emotion lies at the root of intelligent action in the world". He starts the book by slowly demolishing Steven Pinker's notion that "as far as biological cause and effect are concerned, music is useless". For modern Darwinians like Pinker, rallied around the powerful but highly dubious "selfish gene" metaphor, it's perhaps natural that the evolutionary benefits of social cohesion often fall into a blindspot. Mithen makes a convincing case that social cohesion is hugely important in human evolution, that 'emotional intelligence' is central to social bonding, and that music has always been one of our most important methods of expressing emotion and fostering social bonds.

A particularly intriguing thread in this argument is drawn from a 1995 book by eminent historian William H. McNeill: *Keeping it Together: Dance and Drill in Human History*. Mithen quotes from McNeill's account of how his experiences of the apparently senseless repetition of military drills in World War II formed a fertile ground for his later theories:

> *[In time it] somehow felt good … a sense of pervasive well-being is what I recall; more specifically, a strange sense of personal enlargement; a sort of swelling out, becoming bigger than life, thanks to participation in collective ritual.*

In other words, communal music, dance, or even rhythmic marching, *create* as well as reflect a sense of social unity. Of course, we're talking altered states now. But Mithen fails to make the leap: if the induction of this trance can lead to an evolutionarily beneficial "boundary loss" (in McNeill's words), what other methods of trance induction might have played a part in our development? As with *Prehistory of the Mind*, for anyone versed in the basics of the study and/or experience of altered states, the terms of the argument beg this question to be asked.

A lack of concrete archaeological evidence is clearly no obstacle in general for Mithen. He has a fine talent for what might be called "bounded speculation", evolving imaginative theories that are kept within the confines described by available evidence. He reminds us the "absence of evidence is not evidence of absence", and asserts:

> *Although I lack any evidence and doubt if any could be found, I am confident that the music played through the Geissenklösterle pipes [36,000 year-old bone instruments found in Germany] and sung within ice-age painted caves had a religious function.*

I certainly wouldn't argue with that. But the subsequent discussion of religion betrays some rare shoddy thinking, and deepens the mystery as to why hallucinogens are absent from the discussion. He states:

> *Ideas about supernatural beings are the essence of religion. But when such beings cannot be seen, except perhaps during hallucinations, how should one communicate with them?*

It suddenly seems like his anthropological reading has been censored by Harry J. Anslinger![2] There's an easy answer to this question, and he skirts right by it. He quotes a Darwinian professor of religious studies, Matthew Day, as saying "one of the bedevilling problems about dealing with gods is that … they are never really *there*." You can almost see all the shamans looking at him sideways, irate or bemused. The roots of this puzzlement are all too predictable. Mithen says:

Ideas about supernatural beings are unnatural in the sense that they conflict with our deeply evolved, domain-specific understanding of the world. As a consequence they are difficult to hold within our minds and to transmit to others—try, for instance, explaining to someone the concept of the Holy Trinity, or try understanding it when someone explains it to you.

Firstly, the idea that religious ideas conflict with our evolutionary grounding is plain wrong. As Mithen himself argues, religious conceptions were probably the earliest products of the newly evolved "cognitive fluidity". They are our "deeply evolved … understanding of the world", developed over hundreds of thousands of years. Our current conception of "natural" and "supernatural" is a mere froth on the surface of this deep, dark well.

Further, it seems wilfully perverse to use the unfathomable wackiness of Christian theology to argue that humans in the Palaeolithic had problems interacting with the gods. I'm not saying they found their way easily, far from it. I merely think that even a scant survey of initiatory traditions among hunter-gatherers will reveal that many techniques have been developed through our evolution to get around the problem of the gods not being "there". In fact, it was never a problem to get around. Some trance-induction techniques are more gruelling than necking some mushrooms, but the *presence* of gods and spirits is usually far removed from the opaque situation that Christianity and its kin have landed us in. Looking at the immense subtlety of animistic beliefs,[3] and the radically different conception of "supernatural beings" it implies, brings up a wealth of further objections to Mithen's and Day's narrow view of the matter.

THIS IS AN EXCELLENT, even essential book, and it's tempting to be philosophical about the lack of substantial discussion of altered states. I certainly wouldn't kick up any fuss of this nature if I was reading a preliminary paper on a new theory of the

2. The original US "drug czar", whose misinformation campaign against marijuana is legendary.
3. See Graham Harvey's landmark book *Animism: Respecting the Living World*.

THE SINGING NEANDERTHALS   151

origins and music and language. But this is a thick book, painfully close to being comprehensive, and falling short of that mark for no apparent good reason. I look forward to finding someone at Mithen's level who can at least mention the stoned elephant in the middle of the room. In the meantime, with a little customization, his theories will do nicely.

ANDY LETCHER

ff

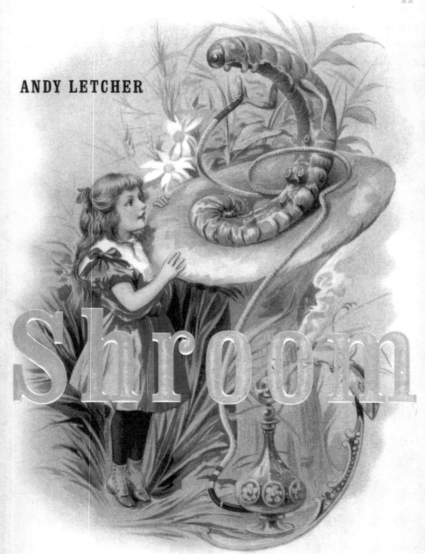

Shroom

a cultural history of the magic mushroom

SHROOM

A CULTURAL HISTORY OF THE MAGIC MUSHROOM

by Andy Letcher

This review was first published on dreamflesh.com in 2007.

S HROOM IS, IN ESSENCE, a big bucket of cold water. Refilled repeatedly, its
sobering crash quells the inflamed romanticism of one theory about psychoactive fungi after another.

In one sense, ploughing through this thoroughly researched and succinctly crafted
survey of the impact of psilocybin and fly agaric mushrooms on human culture becomes,
at times, uncomfortably like watching *Casualty*. Episodes of this BBC hospital drama
invariably begin with characters you've never seen before going about some everyday
business. It's hard to relax into their reality, though, because you know what's coming:
a nasty physical trauma and a dramatic trip to the emergency ward. Here, Letcher
lines up the tantalizing myths surrounding the iconic red-capped *Amanita muscaria*,
the seductively radical theories of people like Gordon Wasson that place psychedelic
plants at the origins of religion, and more. Yet before long you become accustomed to
the dramatic tension of knowing that while one hand gestures with some fascination
towards these beguiling ideas, the other is ready with the pail of icy water.

What prevents *Shroom* from the more objectionable dangers of this relentless type
of cynical dismissal (usually, a repellent smugness that masks its own naivety) is that

Letcher is clearly an "insider". A veteran of the festival and rave culture of the late '80s and early '90s, a one-time fan of Terence McKenna, with a clear fondness for the fungus, he's the kind of guy you want doing your debunking.

There is, it must be said, much to debunk. Gordon Wasson, who brought a surviving Mexican mushroom cult to global attention in the '50s, and dedicated himself to propagating theories about the role of mushrooms in ancient religions, is brought under an especially harsh light. His avowed repugnance at the "hippy trail" that his wake generated in the Oaxacan highlands is carefully turned over to reveal his hidden affinity with this phenomenon, his subtly exploitative interactions with the Mazatec Indians clearly exposed as being far from opposed to the post-colonial "spiritual tourism" of the freaks who descended on the area. John Allegro's infamous *The Sacred Mushroom and the Cross* is easily demolished, the rubble of his theories left shrouded in clouds of doubt about his murky personal motives. And while Terence McKenna is given plenty of leeway (relative to less recent mushroom proselytizers), his dubious Timewave Zero, and many of his prehistorical musings, are in the end cast aside with extreme prejudice.

It's difficult, though, to gain a firm grasp on Letcher's own personal motives. Following the exposition of most of the cherished mycological myths, he prefaces his demolition with something like, "Sadly, this theory does not stand up to scrutiny." There's a genuine tone in this slight sadness. But is it that of someone patiently dismantling a deluded friend's walls of defence, or of someone regretfully sweeping up the detritus of their own youthful over-enthusiasm? There's probably a bit of both.

It would be easy to accuse Letcher of setting up a straw man, in constructing a one-dimensional target of the uncritical hippy, and taking such a person's view as the only proposed route into these slippery speculations in order to flatten it. However, such characters do live and breathe—probably cornering Letcher at parties one time too many.

Also, as Letcher is firmly (though not stridently) in favour of an open, rational approach to mushrooms and other such drugs in current society, one suspects a certain tactical necessity at work. Securing a deal with a major publisher for the "definitive" history of the shroom, it may have been prudent, probably shrewd, to prefix a generally tolerant and positive message with lashings of cold facts.

Even so, there are many problems with the book's approach. It may be true that *Shroom* wasn't the place to address these issues, but they deserve an airing here, at least.

IN A TALK ON GNOSTICISM[1] Erik Davis is asked by a member of the audience (inevitably, the venue being the Burning Man festival) whether psychedelic plants might have been involved in early Gnostic practices. His response is instructive:

What's a better question for me is not, "Is it true?" or "Is it not true?", because they're both boring. [...] We don't know; and that is the place to work. It's in watching yourself want there to be a mushroom hidden in that story—or not. [...] But we don't know. And that "we don't know" is very deep.

"We don't know" is indeed the core thread that runs through Letcher's episodic narrative of dismissal. For all the non-loopy theories—proto-hominids munching African shrooms, European cave painters harvesting Liberty Caps, some nebulous drug cult behind the Indian Soma myth, etc.—there is, after harshly dragging the idea through all the counter-arguments, a concession of, "Well, it may well be the case. But the fact remains, we don't know."

I, like Letcher, was probably "convinced" for a few years in my early twenties by McKenna's theory in *Food of the Gods*, that mushrooms played a vital role in human evolution. But as I delved deeper into prehistorical studies—especially that crucial and compelling arena, the archaeology of rock art—it quickly became apparent that there's no getting away from the bottom line. We don't know. Certain physical information is verifiable, and a number of relatively secure inferences can be constructed atop the meagre tangible remains of early human life; but past that, in the end, we don't know *and can never know*, not for certain.

For me, though, this "don't know" was the starting point for inquiry, not the end point. Keats' "negative capability" ("when man is capable of being in uncertainties, Mysteries, doubts without any irritable reaching after fact & reason") is the baseline. It can be applied as the necessary humility of genuine science (especially in the notoriously shaky social sciences), as much as some vague wishy-washy poetic *state*. It suggests a tolerant appreciation of limits without castrating the irreducible human urge to understand; consideration of multiple models, always with a psychological eye that sees through itself, rather than the search for monolithic "truth". Unfortunately, the pressures of academic careerism and the unsubtle filters that mass media force ideas through tend to exaggerate the latter tendency.

Of course, it is exactly this monolithic approach that Letcher discerns and dismisses in people like Wasson. But, in attacking his theory rather than the general

1. http://www.head-space.us/erikdavis.mp3

cultural ground that feeds both academic orthodoxy and amateur heresies, the power and fertility of "we don't know" is rather lost. His analysis of us wanting there to be "a mushroom hidden in that story" is brilliant and, in the end, quite forgiving. But there's a tendency to use analysis of the modern cultural background to these ideas to *wipe away* their projections into the past, rather than to just loosen their literal solidity a bit while allowing them to still populate our images and narratives of prehistory.

In rounding off his discussion of the important work of David Lewis-Williams and Thomas Dowson on the "trance theory" of prehistoric rock art, Letcher remarks:

> *There are all manner of reasons why people could have been moved to leave patterns and marks upon rocks and stones. Inspired by nature, they might have wanted to draw ripples or waves. Primitive tools might have limited artistic expression to curves and zigzags. Like doodlers everywhere, prehistoric artists might simply have found the patterns pleasing. Or they might have been bored. [...] Academic opinion is at best divided over the model, at worst against it, so once again this particular line of inference reaches a dead end.*

Such quotidian possibilities are always useful to keep to hand when considering these archaic creations. But multiple models doesn't imply a kind of flat relativism where, when considering art that is sometimes found deep in barely accessible tunnels, the "doodling" theory carries equal weight next to the idea of religious trance. Here in particular, Letcher's agenda of debunking seems to have edged him towards allegiance to some highly questionable factions in an academic battle that he sketches with the kind of broad, biased strokes he so often sees in others' work.

And again, rather than framing the theory within a network of models, grounded in doubt but willing to entertain possibilities, he finds "a dead end". "We don't know" is the overt statement, but it's so loaded with cynicism that its ambiguity tends to creak under the weight of outright dismissal. As in archaeology, there is lip service to the maxim that "absence of evidence is not evidence of absence"; but impatience with lack of evidence, and with those who abuse this lack, leaves the pregnant void of unknowing in imminent danger of miscarriage.

SUMMING UP THE ATTEMPTS to identify Soma, that slippery but pervasive figure in psychedelic mythology, Letcher laments: "The hard truth is that, while the search for Soma is diverting, exciting even, it is ultimately futile." Another dead end, and one that fails to see through itself. A key part of Letcher's argument is that our ideas about the mushroom in other cultures say more about ourselves than about anything else. What, though, does this perception of futility reveal? It demonstrates this book's frequent allegiance to (or, at least, blunt use of) the positivist quest for literal truth. Anything short of verifiable certainty (and if we're talking about archaeology and prehistory, that's most of the object of study) seems disappointingly insubstantial.

The sober adherence to documented history itself creates what is basically a fantasy image of the past. The first *recorded* instance of a mushroom's use subtly becomes— however hedged with qualifications about the vast realms of actuality that history inevitably omits—"the first" instance. Letcher fully appreciates the irrepressible nature of the human imagination (this is especially evident in his lucid assessment of the power of the fly agaric to insinuate itself into cultural representations), but as ever, its inevitable role in reifying hard evidence into a fantasy of objective apprehension is left unaddressed in the background.

James Hillman wrote in *Re-Visioning Psychology* that the ego's "specific characteristic, and its specific function, is to represent the literal view: it takes itself and its view for real." He sees the ego as, in the end, just another psychic figure, with its own archetypal background in the Hero—that can-do, literal-minded attitude exemplified by Hercules, who "entered the realm of the shades [Hades] in order to take something, and while he was there he wrestled, he drew his sword, he slaughtered, and was confused about the reality of images." Letcher does a sterling job of exposing the heroic ego at work in the early pioneers who descended into the underworld of prehistory looking to return with concrete, incontrovertible mushrooms; but he also leaves largely in place the Herculean lack of appreciation for the airy liminality of Hades that hard-nosed science constellates.

In playing the science game (which, like the ego, is entirely valid, necessary, but takes itself too literally), Letcher may be judged as betraying his subject. Surely the elven, capricious nature of the psychedelic mushroom, eluding both materialist science and rarified de-fleshed spirituality, deserves an imaginal treatment with some fidelity to its source? In a way, though, the mushroom is honoured. The scoffing cynic won't be confronted with many challenges here, but the probable target audience of the curious or enthused, who have ingested varying amounts of mushroom mythology, may find the relentless debunking as ontologically challenging as any high-dose psilocybin voyage.

FIDELITY TO THE MUSHROOM and appreciation for the positive openings of "we don't know" is one thing; what about intellectual coherence? At the fine level of detail, Letcher is usually impeccable. If anywhere, it is again the scientific suspicion of the broad stroke, the generalization, that trips things up. Introducing his study of myth, *The Two Hands of God*, Alan Watts observed:

> *When the critical intellect looks at anything carefully, it vanishes. This is as true of the solid substance of bodies as of historical generalizations, of entities such as nations, of epochs such as the Middle Ages, and of subject matters such as myth. The reason is, of course, that "things" exists only relatively—for a point of view or for convenience of description. Thus when we inspect any unit more closely we find that its structure is more complex and more differentiated than we had supposed. Its variety comes to impress us more than its unity. This is why there is something of the spirit of debunking in all scholarship and scientific inquiry. As a historian of science once put it, "Isn't it amazing how many things there are that aren't so?"*

This quip may be taken as *Shroom*'s unofficial subtitle! For various reasons, concern for the variety and difference of cultural phenomena is very much the current academic vogue, and distaste for the blunders of the old-school fascination with cross-cultural similarities comes to the fore here in considering Wasson's scholarship. The word "armchair" is invoked to magically banish all traces of credibility, as attempts to grasp the ecology of the cultural forest are rejected in favour of a more botanical adherence to the differences between trees.

Here, the discriminating, micro-level critique of the synthesizing macro perspective is devastatingly accurate, especially in challenging the "cultural evolution" paradigm that informed Wasson's approach to both the "primitive" Mazatecans and the large-scale dynamics of history when considering the mushroom's possible role in the origins of religion. Typically, it misses itself. Its implied narrative describes a history of ideas in which the "primitive" approach of armchair generalists has been soundly defeated, consigned to the rubbish tip of academic history to make way for the more advanced, sophisticated constructionist paradigm. In reality, I sense neither view precludes horrendous mischaracterizations of existence, and any current sense of "progress" will in due course dissolve as some further compensatory shift reveals the folly of prioritizing one scale over the other.

For sure, Lewis Carroll almost certainly didn't base *Alice In Wonderland* on personal psychedelic experience. But in Alice's wisdom, taking a piece of both sides of the mushroom—one to make her bigger and the other to make her smaller—he may have left us a useful general hint about epistemology.

HAVING SAID ALL THAT, I have to end by saying: buy this book. It's an invaluable source of information, much of it previously scattered in obscure publications, and is consistently entertaining and insightful.

Besides, cold dips are bracing. The obvious hit of frigidity makes it easy to forget that in fact a blast of cold water actually stimulates the circulation to warm us up a bit. The excellent final chapter, with its generous affection for mycological ecstasies, has the ambience of a refreshed afterglow. Despite its faults, in the end the book's cold water isn't a repressive crushing of psychedelic passion; rather, it aims to invigorate and refresh. We are wiser for it.

EDWARD C. WHITMONT
RETURN
OF THE GODDESS

THE 21ST CENTURY TRAVELLER IN PREHIST
MEGALITI

JULIAN COPE
THE MODERN
ANTIQUARIAN

THE SPELL OF THE SENSUOUS

Graham Harvey **Animism**
Respecting the Living World

AL ODYSSEY
THIC BRITAIN
300 Prehistoric Sites

DAVID

JULIAN
COPE

PETER LAMBORN WILSON
PLOUGHING THE CLOUDS
The Search for Irish Soma

THE LONG TRIP
A PREHISTORY OF
PSYCHEDELIA
PAUL DEVEREUX

THE
MYTH OF
THE
GODDESS
EVOLUTION
OF AN
IMAGE
ANNE
BARING
AND JULES
CASHFORD

PENGUIN
ARKANA

APPENDIX I
FURTHER READING

Here are a few more books related to the core topics covered in these essays that I've happened across in recent years.

The Spell of the Sensuous: Perception and Language in a More-Than-Human World
by David Abram (Vintage, 1997)

Uses philosophy, anthropology, ecology, linguistics and a potent knack for lyrical prose to weave a convincing re-vision of our mental and bodily relationship to the world around us.

The Myth of the Goddess: Evolution of an Image
by Anne Baring & Jules Cashford (Arkana, 1993)

One of the best surveys of goddesses throughout history, drawing together the latest scholarship against a discreet analytical psychology backdrop to crown and continue the pioneering work of people such as Marija Gimbutas and Joseph Campbell.

The Modern Antiquarian & The Megalithic European
by Julian Cope (Thorsons 1998 & Element 2004)

Essential, mammoth surveys of Neolithic monuments—blasting away antiquarianism's fustiness, and inspiring engagement with pragmatic, exemplary gazetteers.

The Long Trip: A Prehistory of Psychedelia
by Paul Devereux (Arkana, 1997)

One of the best minds studying archaic consciousness turns to documenting our long-term fascination with getting off our tits. Highly readable and full of ideas.

Animism: Respecting the Living World
by Graham Harvey (Hurst, 2005)

The definitive introduction to the "new animism", with a detailed analysis of this complex, misunderstood term, case studies of animist practices both indigenous and modern, and discussions of core animist issues. Recommended.

The Mind in the Cave: Consciousness & The Origins of Art
by David Lewis-Williams (Thames & Hudson, 2002)

Lewis-Williams has no truck with "experiential research", but is a bona fide pioneer of the trance theory of prehistory rock art. This book states the case vividly, with enough caution to stave off all but the wilfully ignorant doubters.

Return of the Goddess
by Edward C. Whitmont (Arkana, 1987)

Whitmont is one of the more interesting Jungians, and here he describes his vision of the cosmic historical drama of the repression and renaissance of the feminine principle. It's slightly stodgy at times, so it's surprising as well as pleasing to find it concluding with an impassioned call for the playful ritualization of sex. Why not?

Ploughing the Clouds: The Search for Irish Soma
by Peter Lamborn Wilson (City Lights, 1999)

An incredibly knotted trail of mythological references fusing meticulous erudition with flights of poetic inspiration. This mercurial search for ecstatic traditions in ancient Ireland is a fascinating, if dense, exercise in throwing in a large net and sorting through the odd fish it hauls up.

APPENDIX II
THE LADDER MOTIF

THE COVER OF THIS BOOK shows a piece of digital art by Andy Hemingway which is inspired by the famous Panorama Stone carvings near Ilkley, West Yorkshire. Along with the Barmishaw Stone, nearby on this craggy northern edge of Rombald's Moor, this petroglyph represents a unique occurrence of "ladder motifs" in British rock art. As my essay 'The Goddess in Wharfedale' shows, I've been as taken by these motifs as anyone, fodder as they are for a "shamanic" reading of cup-and-ring art.

Recently, however, doubt has been cast on the authenticity of the Ilkley ladders. In 2004 the *Ilkley Gazette* reported[1] that Gavin Edwards, a resident archaeologist at the Manor House Museum in Ilkley, had uncovered evidence that potentially inferred that the ladder motifs on the Panorama Stone are a little younger than the rest of the carvings—that they were, in fact, Victorian embellishments.

The story goes that an illustration of the stone's designs from the 1860s bears no trace of the ladders; only later sketches seem to show them. Further, Edwards highlights a report in the *Ilkley Gazette* from March 22nd 1913, describing a lecture by Mr T. C. Gill, Bailiff of Ilkley Moor, in which reference is made to a certain Ambrose Collins, a workman employed at a local convalescent home from 1872-73. Collins was reported to "spend most of his leisure time carving and ornamenting the rocks near the home, evidently hoping that at some future time they would be discovered and become famous."

1. http://archive.ilkleygazette.co.uk/2004/7/16/99012.html

Exception has been taken to this theory;[2] and facts such as the ladders integral to the nearby Barmishaw Stone (right) certainly place it as speculation along with all other theories. But for me, the possibilities it implies raise questions perhaps *equally* interesting to those raised by the idea that the ladder carvings form testimony to some idiosyncratic pre-Roman

The Barmishaw Stone, Rombald's Moor, England

shamanic practices in the region. If Ambrose Collins did indeed add these elements to the Panorama Stone, did he have any inkling he was blending a ubiquitous symbol for shamanic ascent into designs that, as much recent research shows, may already be implicated with vortex-like perceptual phenomena from deep trance states?

It is of course highly unlikely that a Victorian labourer possessed such knowledge of global motifs of the shamanic cosmos. So, why ladders? The hard-nosed scientists are free here to invoke their alibi of choice, "coincidence". However, those who are as interested in the psyche's depths as they are in the comforts of certainty discover here more grist for their mill.

"Doodling" is, like "coincidence", another convenient dismissal for those who see the oceans girding their islands of verifiability as treacherous expanses of irrelevance. A touch of playfulness and respect for uncertainty is always necessary to avoid fruitless pits of questioning, but if these ladders were "doodles"—by prehistoric people or by a Victorian workman—why this image and not another? Shamanic cosmology and the imagery it constellates are frequently specific to the natural and cultural ecology of the tradition in question; yet in other important respects it emerges from the deepest, most universal levels of human being. The "form constants" of the trance theory of rock art, thought to arise from the structure of the optic nerve, seem to me to be the tip of an iceberg where our shared physiology merges seamlessly into our overlapping psychic foundations. The templates for experience encoded in these deeper levels of our psychophysical make-up are as likely to nudge and steer the hand of an absent-minded doodler as they are to govern the unfolding of visions in a shaman whose everyday mind has been forcibly absented by trance induction techniques.

Whichever way the mystery is sliced, it seems happy to confirm for the open-

2. For instance, see http://www.ilkleyrocks.com/?p=653

minded investigator its evocative irreducibility.

THE LADDER APPEARS in other European rock art, most notably in the richly endowed region of Val Camonica in northern Italy. The mostly Bronze and Iron Age petroglyphs here are already unfathomably linked to the moors around Ilkley thanks to the identity of form found between the famed Swastika Stone and the Camunian Rose motifs (see p. 84). In some instances (e.g. the carving shown here) ladders apparently lead up to vortex-like places that resonate strongly with the structure of the Ilkley cup-and-ring designs.

Iron Age carving, Val Camonica, Italy

However, many of the Italian carvings have been shown to relate directly to the style of wooden dwelling known to have been common in the region at the time the petroglyphs were being carved. This photo of a beautiful recent reconstruction doesn't directly show the ladders (they're tucked away to the left of the picture). However, it's clear that we may have here a more "mundane" explanation for the Camunian ladders.

The problem with this reasoning, following as it does the reflexive hidden narrative of debunking that's as seductive as any urge to romanticize, is that it's based on a relatively recent conception of the mundane/numinous polarity. Examples of tradi-

Reconstructed Iron Age dwelling, Val Camonica, Italy

tional cultures imbuing details of their everyday lives, large and small, with complex, profoundly resonant links to their cosmology and spiritual beliefs are too common to catalogue here. Mircea Eliade remarks in *The Sacred and the Profane*:

... the symbolism of the center is the formative principle not only of countries, cities, temples, and palaces but also of the humblest human dwelling, be it the tent of a nomad hunter, the shepherd's yurt, or the house of the sedentary cultivator.

The recent flurry of secularism in human history likes to picture itself as the latest and highest rung on an evolutionary ladder. Certainly the concept of secularism is a useful tool in these pluralistic times; but I wonder whether we should find common ground *within* the religious sphere as well as outside it. The imaginal ladder that beckons from the psychic topography mapped by the shaman hints at something more useful, and less arrogant, than the evolutionary ladder brandished by those who misinterpret Darwin.

John Gray writes in *Black Mass*: "The most necessary task of the present time is to accept the irreducible reality of religion." This has little to do with a resignation to the mass insanity of monotheism. Rather, it calls on us to excavate the experiences, patterns, and symbols—fixed or mutable—that inform the endless permutations of the human imagination, and to breathe animate life into them.

INDEX

STRANGE ATTRACTOR

JOURNAL THREE

○ ARABIC ALCHEMY ○ OPIUM DEMONS ○ VIRGIL AS NECROMANCER ○
○ THEOSOPHICAL THOUGHTFORM ART ○ PSYCHOACTIVE ANIMALS ○
○ EXTRA-UTERINE BIRTHS ○ BURMA'S SPIRIT POSSESSION FESTIVAL ○
○ A VICTORIAN TIME MACHINE ○ LIVERPOOL'S TUNNELLING PHILANTHROPIST ○
○ XAVIER FORNERET ○ ELECTROCHEMICAL ARTWORKS ○ STEWART HOME: ARTIST ○
○ THE UNSEEN HANS CHRISTIAN ANDERSEN ○ REDONDA AND HER KINGS ○
○ THE HOUSE OF DOLLS ○ MARTIN DENNY ○ KOESTLER'S DIRTY THIRTIES ○

JOURNAL TWO

○ MY TRAVELS WITH MUNCHAUSEN ○ PSYCHEDELIC RITES OF ANCIENT PERU ○
○ THE HALIFAX SLASHER ○ THE TEMPLE AT THE END OF TIME ○ WILFRIED SATTY ○
○ HOMONCULI AND GOLEMS ○ ROBOT PRIDE ○ MOULD ART ○ UNDER PETTICOAT RULE ○
○ ON THE USE OF DEAD BABIES ○ BORIS VIAN ○ MAYA DEREN ○ RICHARD JEFFERIES ○
○ LOKI: THE PERVERT GOD ○ CF RUSSELL AND THE I CHING ○ ANIMIST MANIFESTO ○
○ THE NIGHT TERROR ○ BRAIN FUNGUS ○ FOLKLORE OF UNDERGROUND LONDON ○
○ ADMIRAL BYRD'S FLIGHT TO ATLANTIS ○ ALCHEMY AT THE ROYAL SOCIETY ○
○ NEPALESE SCHOOL FOR SHAMANS ○ WALDO SABINE AT THE COURT OF LUST ○

CELEBRATING UNPOPULAR CULTURE

ANTHROPOLOGY, PSYCHOLOGY, ETHNOGRAPHY, MAGICK, ARTS,
LITERATURE, LOST HISTORIES, REJECTED SCIENCE, LANDSCAPE, LIFE

AVAILABLE AT DISCERNING BOOK SHOPS
AND DIRECT FROM WWW.STRANGEATTRACTOR.CO.UK

DREAMFLESH

A Journal of Ecological Crisis & Archaeologies of Consciousness

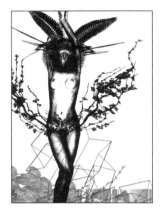

VOLUME I ~ AUTUMN 2006

Featuring: Origin theories ~ *Ayahuasca* initiation ~ Ancestor magic ~ Breathwork myths ~ Peak Oil ~ Sacramental food ~ Apocalypse dreams

With: PETER LAMBORN WILSON ~ STEPHEN GRASSO ~ MICHAEL ORTIZ HILL ~ DONAL RUANE ~ RICHARD HEINBERG ~ ORRYELLE DEFENESTRATE-BASCULE ~ DAVE LEE

Includes: A3 full-colour poster by PABLO AMARINGO & original cover art by AMODALI

"I felt *excited* as I read. No mean feat. I truly was inspired."
— GENESIS BREYER P-ORRIDGE

"A bastion of the esoteric."
— THE GUARDIAN

To order a copy, send your address and a sterling cheque for £8 (UK), or £9 (Rest of World) payable to 'Dreamflesh' to the address below (prices include post & packing). Or order securely online at http://dreamflesh.com/journal/one

---

VOLUME II ~ DUE SPRING 2008

Featuring: Interviews with DOUGLAS RUSHKOFF, PATRICK HARPUR & DAVID KIDNER ~ AMODALI ~ BITSY BROUGHTON on working with animals in dreams ~ JASON GODESKY on the ecology of the imagination ~ DAVID LUKE & MARIOS KITTENIS on cutting-edge parapsychology research ~ GORDON MACLELLAN ~ MARK PILKINGTON on animal intelligence ~ DAVID SCHOEN on the psychic impact of Hurricane Katrina ~ Art by ANDREW GONZALEZ

BM 2374, London, WC1N 3XX, UK ~ http://dreamflesh.com